SAFE YOUNG DRIVERS

A Guide for Parents and Teens

Phil Berardelli

AskPhil@SafeYoungDrivers.com

Nautilus Communications, Inc.

Vienna, Virginia

Library of Congress Cataloging-in-Publication Data

Berardelli, Phil.
    Safe young drivers: a guide for parents and teens / Phil
Berardelli.
        p. cm.
    Includes index.
    ISBN 0-9675191-4-4
        1. Automobile driver education.   2. Teenage automobile
    drivers — education.   I. Title.
    TL 152.6.B47   2000
    629.28'3 — DC20   Number pending
                                                    CIP

Nautilus Communications, Inc.
    P.O.Box 1600
    Vienna, VA 22183-1600
Printed in Canada

First edition, October 1996
Second edition, November 2000

Book and cover design by Tom Huestis

Drawings by F. A. Berardelli

Author photograph by Barbara Freeman

For Angela and Melissa

FOREWORD

Being the author of *Safe Young Drivers* has been both a rewarding and surprisingly challenging experience for me. When I first published the book in 1996, I had intended it to be a relatively straightforward tool for self-help. But now, four years later, it has evolved into something of a personal crusade. This is due in large part to the countless hours I've spent discussing driving issues with parents and teens. Much of what I've learned from those discussions hasn't been encouraging.

I find that many parents still give in too easily to pressure from their children to obtain licenses on or near their sixteenth birthdays. Reluctantly or eagerly, many nevertheless hand over the keys to their inadequately-trained kids. They also believe it's okay to buy vehicles for teens right away — too often, flashy and powerful vehicles.

Some parents even support beginning the teaching process as early as fifteen. They rationalize the decision by arguing that they're giving kids extra time to learn, and therefore it will make them better young drivers.

But in four years, the facts remain undeniable. Vehicle crashes still claim more teen lives than any other cause. For the youngest drivers — the ones for whom this book was written — the death toll is actually increasing. Each day that you spend using this book, 20 teens, on average, will die on our highways. More than 1,500 will be injured, some disabled for life.

Even worse, teens driving teens is a recipe for disaster. A recent study by Johns Hopkins University revealed that sixteen-year-old drivers carrying one passenger are 39 percent more likely to die in a crash than when driving alone. That figure jumps to 86 percent with two passengers, and 182 percent with three or more. Seventeen year olds fare just as badly.

All this information confirms that *Safe Young Drivers* is needed just as much now as the day it was published. It is more than just a useful tool. It is a weapon to help you deal with a life-and-death issue.

On the positive side, many of my encounters with parents and teens have provided useful feedback, which I have used to improve and update the book. For example, this new edition includes a 10-page Lesson Log. I added it to help parents keep better track of those 100 hours of behind-the-wheel instruction that I recommend. The log begins on page 163. It can be part journal, part reminder and, when it's complete, a memento of all your hard work.

Also in response to requests, I've expanded the section called "Choosing a Car for Your Teen," beginning on page 143. And in the "Reviews and Resources" section, beginning on page 173, I've included a list of other useful publications and Web sites related to teen driving topics.

Following the wisdom of my friends in the highway safety community, I've stopped using the term "accidents." The National Highway Traffic Safety Administration has been urging everyone to do this for several years. "Crashes Aren't Accidents," according to NHTSA. That's right. Almost every motor vehicle collision is caused by human error.

Finally, I've modified some of my recommendations to reflect new research, new "best practices" wisdom, or new vehicle features. Some things have changed, and I want to keep *Safe Young Drivers* as up-to-date as possible.

I hope you will find this book useful, and I hope you will send me your comments and questions via the Web site:
www.SafeYoungDrivers.com

I especially appreciate hearing from people who've used the book, and I'll continue to post the most relevant questions on the "Ask Phil" page. By all means, please tell others about the book. Let's keep working to reduce the number of teens dying needlessly on our roads and highways.

Drive safely. Be a Lightfoot!
Phil

CONTENTS

FOREWORD   2

HOW TO USE THIS BOOK   6
    Ten Lessons, Five Themes   7

INTRODUCTION FOR PARENTS   8

INTRODUCTION FOR TEENS   14

GETTING STARTED   20
    The First Question to Ask: Is Your Child Ready?   20
    The Learner's Permit   23
    Before the Vehicle is Moved   24
    A Few Words About Teaching   26
    The Best Place to Start   29

THE FIRST DAY   30
    The Pre-Drive Checklist   30
    Getting a Grip   32
    Theme One of Five: CLEAR THE WAY   33
    Clean and Clear   34

TEN STEPS TO BASIC SKILLS   35
    1. Basic Moves   36
    2. Back Roads, Quiet Streets   42
    3. Busy but Slow Encounters   51

4. Stop and Go   56

5. Countryside   67

    Theme Two of Five: LEARN THE LIMITS   70

    Theme Three of Five: SHARE THE ROAD   79

6. Getting Up to Highway Speeds   85

7. Night Driving   103

8. City Streets   107

    Theme Four of Five: THINK AHEAD   108

9. Into Heavy Traffic   111

10. Coping With Bad Weather   121

    Theme Five of Five: FEEL THE ROAD   128

ON TO THE LICENSE (and then what?)   139

    Sensible Limits for Young Drivers   139

    Post-License Checkups   141

    You Still Can Say "No"   142

    Choosing a Car for Your Teen   143

ONE MORE THING   145

SOME ABC'S FOR THE ROAD   147

INDEX   156

ACKNOWLEDGMENTS   160

ABOUT THE AUTHOR   162

LESSON LOGS   163

REVIEWS AND RESOURCES   173

HOW TO USE THIS BOOK

In this video and computer age, books seem to occupy a less important role in our daily lives. That's sad, although it is a reality of modern society and a matter of personal preference. Sometimes, however, books can be very useful. Driving instruction is one such time.

The best place to learn how to drive is on the road, not in front of a TV screen or computer monitor. Good skills and road sense only develop through repeated and lengthy exposure to real situations and sensations. Information about driving is most valuable when it can accompany you.

Although both parent and teen should read through the book before you get started, keep the book in the vehicle during the lessons. The large type makes it easy to read even if you're moving — as a passenger, not a driver. The book is sized to fit conveniently into the glove compartment. And the spiral binding allows you to keep a specific page open easily.

Certain sections of the book are intended for parents, while other sections are for teens. There's also a crossover. Teens can't use the book while they're driving, so they must study the sections that apply to them ahead of time and thoroughly. Parents should help them through those sections during the lessons.

The lessons are broken down as much as possible into simple steps, but there is a lot to remember. Parents and teens should refer to the book often. There's an effective way to do this. It's called Brief/Perform/Debrief. Here's how it works:

—Before a driving session begins, both parties should read through the relevant text.

—During the lesson, the parent or instructor should refer to the text frequently to make sure all the material is being covered and performed correctly.

— After the lesson, both parties should spend a few minutes talking over how the session went. Did the teen understand everything? Were there difficulties?

A pre-printed lesson log is included in the back of this book. Use it to keep track of the material covered and the teen's progress and problems.

Last, when all the lessons have been completed, keep the book in the vehicle, for quick reference whenever necessary. This may sound like a shameless promotion, but you never know when it may come in handy.

TEN LESSONS, FIVE THEMES

Though this book is about acquiring driving skills, it's also about learning and maintaining a good attitude about driving. In fact, as we'll discuss later, good attitude may be even more important than good skills. This is true especially during the early driving years, when those skills are still developing. Inexperience can be dangerous on today's roads. But good attitude can compensate for the lack of skills. That's why, in addition to ten steps, there are five basic themes — approaches — to driving that should be learned. They are introduced at appropriate times and appear at various places in the text.

The five themes are:
- CLEAR THE WAY
- LEARN THE LIMITS
- SHARE THE ROAD
- THINK AHEAD
- FEEL THE ROAD

The themes will appear in capital letters whenever they are included in the text because they represent important information. As the specifics of the individual lessons fade into the past, the themes should linger in the memory. Parents and teens should try hard to retain them.

INTRODUCTION FOR PARENTS

If you're like most parents, a moment comes sooner or later for you when your child makes a declaration of independence. Through word or deed, your offspring announces that your parental preeminence is over.

A typical statement:

Mom, Dad, you're so twenty years ago!

Or:

You just don't understand me!

Or that ultimate insult:

You're so uncool!

Whatever. The message is clear. No more idolizing their parents. No more public displays of affection. In fact, no more public anything, unless it's absolutely necessary.

The inevitable and traumatic event usually arrives when kids reach age twelve or thirteen, sometimes earlier, a natural part of the process by which a child matures sooner or later into an adult. During that period — within which teenagers seem to occupy a universe unto themselves — the parent-child relationship becomes a frequently tense, occasionally explosive tug of war. You may attempt to teach and guide and lead, just as you have been doing all along. But suddenly, your child isn't listening anymore. You might even begin to wonder whether he or she has been secretly kidnapped by aliens and replaced with a look-alike monster!

I was constantly reminded of this phenomenon not only in my own household, but also during the seven years in the 1980s when I was a teacher of seventh and eighth graders. It was a great time, some of the most fun I've ever had. I liked my students and, mostly, they liked me.

Once in a while, one of them would even confide, "Mr. B.," (they used to call me) "You're so cool. Not like my parents. They're awful!"

Whenever I'd receive such a compliment, I'd politely thank my young suitor and reply with an invitation:

"Come over to my house. I want you to tell my kids what you just told me."

The remark usually brought an expression of befuddlement from the student. But any parent would understand the irony immediately. My own children, of course, were not congratulating me on my coolness. To the contrary, it was all I could do to get them to listen to me. To be seen in public with me would lead to their profound embarrassment. After all, I was their "Da-yad!"

There is a brief time, however, when this seemingly endless ordeal subsides. It usually happens around age fifteen. That's when your child seems suddenly not so defiant, argumentative, or stubborn. In fact, he or she actually begins to pay a little more attention to you.

It may take you a while to catch on, but your teen has been thinking ahead. He or she has realized that those dreaded parents now possess something very desirable: permission. Permission to begin driving.

Among modern teens, the quest for a driver's license is the equivalent of The Holy Grail. They can pursue it with fervor. At last, no more being driven around by a parent! Besides, _all_ their friends are driving. At least, that's what they claim.

So begins a new wrinkle in the parent-child relationship. Kids cajole, promise, and bargain — perhaps even argue logically and responsibly. More likely tactics are sulking, moaning, pouting, stomping, crying, and maybe yelling, whatever it takes to obtain a learner's permit at the earliest possible time.

In too many cases, the strategy works. Parents get worn down by the constant barrage. Children have the desire and lots of time — a powerful combination. They often win against a parent's better judgment.

9

"I just can't take the nagging" is a common excuse.

"All their friends _are_ driving" is another one.

"I'd rather have _them_ driving than their friends" is yet another.

And, the old standard: "I just don't have the time to chauffeur them everywhere."

But I don't sympathize.

There are many issues that can bring parents and teens into conflict. Drinking, drugs, sex and entertainment are common flashpoints. All require a high degree of parental responsibility and guidance.

Driving is different. It is the one area of modern life over which parents have been granted absolute authority. No one under eighteen may obtain a learner's permit or driver's license anywhere in the United States without parental permission. Children may protest all they want. But they may not operate an automobile without the written consent of a parent or guardian.

You may dread the issue, but _you_ must make the decision. You are legally responsible, and state governments have been wise to make you so. Consider just this one statistic: Sixteen-year-old drivers are likely to be involved in vehicle crashes _up to twelve times_ as often as any other age group. Although traffic deaths have declined substantially over the past twenty years, sixteen is still by far the most dangerous age for drivers.

According to the Insurance Institute for Highway Safety, which has studied the subject for many years, motor vehicle crashes constitute the single largest health problem for sixteen-to-nineteen-year-olds in the United States. They account for more than one-third of all deaths in this group, and a similar share of injuries.

None of this should come as a surprise. Anyone who is even moderately aware of the issue knows that the youngest drivers have the most crashes. While I was writing this book, one rainy spring afternoon, a sixteen-year-old in a light pick-up truck smacked into my parked car. The damage was minor, and the youngster was not injured, but the experience is very, very common.

A few years before that, I was driving near my home in Northern Virginia. As I approached an intersection, a young man swerved around a corner and smashed into me. He had lost control of his car. He also was sixteen and had been driving only a few months. I ended up with a sore neck and a bump on my head, and he was somewhat traumatized. Otherwise we both were okay.

Others have not been so lucky. The news too frequently contains tragic stories involving young drivers. The challenge is how to get them through their first years unscathed. After age eighteen, the odds begin to improve — slowly.

Yet in the U.S., drivers' licenses may be obtained at a younger age than in most other industrialized, traffic-clogged nations. Learners' permits currently are not required in 18 states, and only 15 states require them to be held for minimum periods — usually no more than 90 days — before young drivers are eligible for licenses.

These thoughts were uppermost in my mind when I taught my own children to drive. Unlike my own youth — in rural Western Pennsylvania, where a childhood friend and I learned the nuances of a standard transmission in an ancient Studebaker, bumping over fields and little-traveled dirt roads — the vast majority of us today live in densely-populated areas, where main arteries are multi-laned highways with speed limits of 65 miles an hour or more.

It's unfortunate, but we cannot rely upon driver education classes or commercial driving establishments to inculcate our children. Year after year, school programs are subjected to funding cutbacks and they are not nearly thorough enough. Commercial instruction these days is expensive and, all too often, inadequate.

11

Most state driving exams tend to concentrate on rules and regulations. They require very little in the way of real driving skills. Parallel parking seems to be a major component, for instance. License requirements remain as undemanding as they were years and years ago, when the volume of motor vehicle traffic was only a fraction of what it is now. In my own state, Virginia, the driver's manual devotes only a dozen pages to safe driving techniques. Clearly, state governments and local school districts are, by and large, not providing the ideal instructional environment where driving is concerned.

These are not very satisfactory circumstances, but there is a remedy: Do what I did. Teach your child yourself. I know it might sound daunting. After all, turning a gangly, sassy, normal teenager into a skilled and responsible driver, who can maneuver up to two tons of vehicle safely in traffic, in all kinds of weather, is no casual activity.

On the other hand, it can be done. It requires two essential ingredients: dedication and time. Any parent who is willing to give both can become the best possible instructor.

This book is meant to help you do just that. It encompasses everything I have learned about the process. It is structured to help anyone who is willing to take on the task. It is a common-sense approach, intended to provide you with the basic information you need to teach your child well.

It is also a developmental, step-by-step approach. You begin simply, and proceed carefully through increasingly complex tasks. The student masters each set of skills before moving on. You don't need the expertise of a race car driver to provide a firm foundation. Even at highway speeds, the basic skills described herein can produce a safe and competent driver, _if_ they are practiced consistently and given time to develop.

Time is the critical factor. How much time? A lot — about 100 hours. But there are many ways to approach this task. It doesn't have to be overwhelming. For one thing, you can tailor the instruction to fit your schedule. For another, no matter what you do, your child's mind and body will need time to develop and mature. The lessons must be absorbed. Habits take time to appear. This is something you should not hurry. And some of the instruction can continue _after_ the license is obtained.

That's right. There are aspects of driving that shouldn't be attempted too early. The basic skills must be ingrained before more complex tasks are undertaken. You need to approach the time requirement the same way you approach the lessons: go step by step.

Do what you can when you can. If you have an hour or so each day to devote to lessons, for example, set aside that time and work with your teen every day. If you can only work on this a couple of times a week, that can be a valid approach, too.

However you structure it, commit to the overall process. Commit to the idea that you will teach your child. Then, everything else becomes detail and variation.

Consider also that this can be a pleasant and valuable experience. It can allow you to return briefly to being the center of your teen's attention. Imagine, being out in public without the complaining! That's what happens when a teen gets to sit in the driver's seat.

I remember vividly the times when I taught my two daughters. Right away, I noticed they began exhibiting a strange mellowing quality. It wasn't a giant swing, by any means. But I had become accustomed to constant and vigorous resistance about so many things — parties, dating, music, clothing — that my nerves had been rubbed raw enough to be sensitive to the change.

As we progressed through the weeks and months of the instruction, there was a definite shift in our relationships. My girls stopped being instinctively hostile to me, and I began to regard them as young adults instead of children.

Most of the time, we had fun together. It was a welcome change. It can work for you. It can become a time of renewed bonding between you and your teen. It can help you adjust to your child's growing sense of independence. And it presents your youngster with an opportunity to demonstrate maturity and judgment.

Remember also that driving is not just a process of skills but of values, such as courtesy, common sense and even helpfulness. Teaching your child to drive can be a very effective way to communicate those values. Above all, it can give your young driver a better chance on the highways and make him or her less of a danger to anyone else. That's something worth all the time in the world.

INTRODUCTION FOR TEENS

If you want to drive well, you're going to need good skills. But this book is about more than that. It's also meant to encourage you to adopt a good *attitude* about driving — an attitude that's environmentally and socially conscious as well as safe.

Believe me, good attitude is even more important than good skills. That's because good attitude will *always* help you avoid situations that your skills, no matter how sharp, can't overcome.

Over the years, you may have gotten used to seeing driving portrayed in a certain way. In the movies, for example, or in car commercials. You know what I mean. Drivers are seen roaring down roads — or, in the case of sport-utility vehicles, literally tearing up the landscape. The actors in the commercials are attractive young adults. Maybe the vehicle is a convertible or has a sunroof. Rock music blares on the soundtrack.

A European carmaker has run an ad on TV in which a young woman careens through the streets of a city in her little red coupe, commenting that she needs to cut down on caffeine. Another ad by the same carmaker shows a pair of young parents and their small kids, also zooming down a road, leaving dust in their wake. Many other manufacturers employ the same tactics. The message is clear: buy our car so you can drive fast and be cool! No traffic, no worries.

But behavior like that has consequences, not just in terms of life and limb. Aggressive driving causes more pollution, noise, wear and tear on the vehicle, erosion of the pavement and the land, and danger to animal life as well as human. Put those glamorous images out of your mind. They don't represent the reality of the roadways.

I'd like you to think about this a little before you begin your instruction. I'd like you to do something as well. If you can, take a walk near a busy highway, such as on an overpass of a freeway — anywhere there is a lot of traffic. Then spend some time watching all the vehicles go by. Listen to the amount of noise the traffic produces. Notice how relentless the procession is. And be aware of the effect just being near all that traffic is having on you.

Not a very pretty or pleasant place to be, is it? _That's_ the reality of cars and highways. Every time I'm near a source of traffic, I always feel like every vehicle is somehow assaulting me. I can feel its noise and velocity beating on my chest. It makes me very uneasy. I feel even more uneasy whenever I walk along roads and streets where the traffic is frequent or constant. My urge always is to get away from the noise and commotion as soon as I can. I want peace and quiet.

You have to do this once in a while. Observe traffic from the perspective of the surrounding environment. You can't experience this from inside a vehicle.

When you begin your driving lessons, there's something else you may notice as you mix with traffic: the large number of aggressive drivers on the road. These are people who tend to regard driving as a competition. They are always trying to get ahead of everyone else. They swerve in and out of lanes. They pass on the right. They seldom stop at stop signs and they zip through red lights at every opportunity. Heaven help anybody who cuts them off or blocks their way.

Suddenly, the behavior you see displayed in commercials doesn't seem so glamorous. It seems stupid and dangerous. Yet these individuals are not strangers or foreigners or aliens. They are people who live all around you. Aggressive driving is a pervasive and nasty national habit.

It's not confined to crowded highways. Aggressive ones continue their habits along many sidestreets or secondary roadways. I live in a suburban neighborhood of cul-de-sacs connected by a two-lane road with a 25-mile-an-hour speed limit. I go walking or jogging along that road every morning. I see very few people obeying the speed limit. It doesn't seem to matter to them that they are zooming through a neighborhood, where people walk, children play, and pets and wild creatures roam.

While I was writing this book, usually early in the morning, I listened to the radio — public affairs radio (yeah, I know, I'm a dull guy). Several times an hour, a local traffic report would come on. There was always a collision somewhere in the area, stopping traffic and causing misery for its victims. Such incidents almost always involved somebody who was driving aggressively. Aggression means speed, and speed causes most crashes. Of course, if you add alcohol, it creates an even more frightening and dangerous situation.

You'll be hearing a lot about all this in the coming months, possibly from your driver's ed. instructor, your department of motor vehicles, or from other sources. I won't belabor the subject, but I would like you to consider just a few things:

— First, as a teenager, you are more likely to die in an automobile than anywhere else, whether you are the driver or a passenger. That's not to say it _will_ happen. Although the odds are very small — about 13 chances in 100,000 if you're a male and about 6 in 100,000 if you're a female — the danger is real.

— Second, if you make it through your first three years as a driver, your survival odds will improve substantially. That's important to remember. It means that you must be extra careful during your early years as a driver, because that's when you are most vulnerable to death and injury.

— Third, and this is something you may not have heard before, even if you have acquired very good driving skills, they will not necessarily lower the odds of your having a serious crash during your teen years. It's a little known fact, but it's true. There have been several studies of this phenomenon, and they all have reached the same conclusion. Why? Researchers aren't certain, but their best guess is that good driving skills don't prevent crashes unless they are accompanied by good driving behavior.

Teens have a natural tendency to take risks. Driving fast is risky. But it is also an exhilarating experience. Yes, it can be fun!

Here's where the danger comes in, even for skilled young drivers: Instead of remaining cautious and tentative, as they should while they're still learning, many teens use

17

their newfound freedom behind the wheel to test limits. They barrel down highways, whip in and out of lanes, and challenge other drivers, especially other teens. They become instant aggressors. And quite often, alcohol enters the picture.

You know the rest. You also know this is true. If you're in high school, you've seen it all around you.

You should also know, if you didn't already, that males are more than twice as likely to have serious crashes as females. But while the crash total for males has been declining over the past 20 years, the total for females has been rising. More and more female drivers are taking to the roads as aggressively as males — and paying a price for their risky behavior.

That's why it's extremely important that you develop the right attitude toward driving, along with good skills. Skills will only take you so far. When things go bad on the road, they can go bad very, very quickly. You can find yourself suddenly in a situation you can't handle. No matter how good you think you are, many driving hazards can overwhelm you. Only the proper attitude will help you avoid those hazards before they arise.

— Fourth, while there are many things in your life that are your business — what you think, how you dress, who you like, the music you listen to — driving is different. Driving is something you do on public roads, sharing space with lots of other people of different ages and viewpoints. What they do affects you, and what you do affects them.

I'm not telling you any of this to discourage you from driving, or to make you feel depressed. I'm not even trying to spoil your fun. But driving doesn't have to be dangerous to be fun. You can enjoy it just as much by doing it well, by knowing what to do in just about every situation, and by improving the safety of the roadway, not reducing it.

I want to try to raise your consciousness, to give you a heightened awareness about what driving in America really means today. I want to give you a healthy, positive approach to being behind the wheel.

So please consider carefully all the material contained in this book. Be patient and accept the instruction that your parent or guardian will attempt to give you. Take the time to allow your skills to develop into habits.

As long as you are involved in the learning process, stick to the practices I have outlined. Later on, you may decide you want to depart from them. They may seem too tame for you. Or, you may choose other ways of doing things that suit you better.

But let me assure you: What you learn here, if practiced consistently, will never let you down. The techniques are solid. The attitude will help you to travel lightly, safely and enjoyably along the roads and through neighborhoods. And together they will help prevent you from doing harm to yourself or anyone else. That's a goal worth striving for.

GETTING STARTED

THE FIRST QUESTION TO ASK:
IS YOUR CHILD READY?

I'll say it at the outset. My personal opinion is that few if any teenagers are ready to drive with no restrictions at age sixteen. It is a major risk to allow them onto today's highways.

Furthermore, the statistics are undeniable. Sixteen is the most dangerous age for drivers, followed closely by seventeen and eighteen. Yet year after year, many parents routinely allow their kids to obtain learners' permits even before they reach sixteen. Some are taken for their licenses on their birthdays, as if the age automatically qualified them to drive. Granted, many states allow learner's permits to be obtained at age fifteen and will issue licenses on sixteenth birthdays. But that doesn't make it right.

It is a mistake to assume that your state knows best for your child. On today's dangerous highways, inexperience and poor judgment are frequently a lethal combination. Driving is a critical area where your maturity and concern should prevail. Not outmoded state regulations. Not peer pressure.

There seems to be a widespread attitude of resignation among parents. Let the kids have their licenses, ready or not, and hope for the best. In most cases, nothing dramatic or tragic happens. Maybe there's a fender-bender or two, but no worse. Good fortune wins over good sense.

I am convinced this is not a sound approach. Too many children are harmed because they simply do not understand how much power they are attempting to control when they get behind the wheel. Or, they have not been trained properly so they put themselves into situations they cannot overcome when things go wrong. Or, as so many kids do, they believe they cannot be harmed, so despite the skills they have learned they risk themselves — and sometimes their passengers.

That's the key thing to remember here: most of the time, nothing happens, but when something does, either it's too late to help or the young driver's skills are insufficient. Usually, it's both. Good driving habits are very easy to learn. They simply must be practiced, repeatedly. They must also be accompanied by good judgment, which takes time to develop.

Most important, driving skills cannot be used properly unless they are reflexive. You can't think about evasive actions while you're executing them. It takes too long. When needed, skills must be automatic. And they can only become automatic by practicing them, over and over, for months and months and months. *There is no other way.*

Think of playing a musical instrument. You can't sit down at the piano and perform like an expert right away. It takes time to read the music, to learn technique, to strengthen the muscles guiding the hands and the fingers, to develop senses of rhythm and emphasis. When you learn to play a melody, you no longer think about the individual notes. Instead, your fingers feel the sequence. They move faster than you can think. The skill displayed by playing well is performed by a different part of the brain than conscious thinking.

Driving works the same way. If you had to think about every single thing you were doing, you would be tense constantly. You would become fatigued quickly. For example, whenever you drive through thick fog or rain or snow, especially at night, you tend to search every foot of the road almost frantically for a sudden obstruction or change. Time seems to slow down. It takes forever to go anywhere. Your muscles tense. Your heart rate elevates. You have a general feeling of unease. After a brief time, you become very tired.

On the other hand, if the weather is clear and visibility is good, especially on a roadway frequently traveled, you are at ease. You don't exert conscious effort. Just like playing a well-practiced tune on the piano, driving is performed automatically. It's second nature.

With this in mind, I argue that it's impossible for someone who has just turned sixteen to have good driving skills. There has not been enough time for those skills to appear. And if a teenager doesn't have good skills, what is he or she doing on the road? This is why I believe all parents must decide, not whether their child is ready to drive at sixteen, but whether the child is ready to _learn_ to drive.

In my own case, I faced a different situation with each of my daughters. My firstborn was ready at sixteen — to learn. She was a very bright kid, very level-headed, mature for her age. She possessed the mental discipline needed to learn the rules of the road quickly. She could focus her attention and listen carefully. She had excellent hand-eye coordination. She had been a ballet dancer. She was a fair athlete.

Shortly after her sixteenth birthday we went to the DMV and acquired her learner's permit. About six months later, after almost daily instruction and practice, she obtained her license.

My younger daughter presented me with a difficult dilemma. She, too, was a bright kid. Also compassionate, caring, fun to be with. But there were certain things, at that stage of her development, that worried me: She was late frequently. She had trouble staying organized—both in her schoolwork and in her personal life. She also was somewhat forgetful, and she was a little uncoordinated when she played sports.

None of these things was serious, and all are common traits in a developing teen. But driving demands concentration and control. If my daughter's physiological development didn't yet meet the requirements of driving—in my judgment—then as a responsible parent I would have to make her wait. It wasn't easy, because I knew it would hurt her feelings. Nevertheless, I did it. She didn't obtain her license until after her eighteenth birthday.

As a consolation for the wait, I bought her a car, a 1975 Oldsmobile Cutlass Supreme, with a massive steel frame and 16-inch wheels — a tank. She learned to drive in this behemoth and kept it for a year after she obtained her license. During that time, she had three collisions, all minor but nevertheless her fault. She has had none in the twelve years since. I am certain that had she been driving at a younger age, her total would have been higher.

The two-year delay became a trying time for both of us. But I remain convinced that I made the right decision. I am grateful that her early mishaps were not more serious. I feel deeply for parents who have had to deal with the worst.

This is not to say that everyone should be made to wait. It's just that I want to encourage all parents with driving age teens to approach this subject with care and contemplation. There may be no simple criteria for making this decision. But if you determine that your child is not ready, if he or she has not yet exhibited the necessary level of attention, maturity or self-disipline, there is a simple answer. It is a two-word answer, very difficult to utter, but perhaps the most important, loving, caring words you can say: "Not yet."

THE LEARNER'S PERMIT

As already mentioned, not all states require a learner's permit before a driver's license. In fact, a recent survey by the Insurance Institute for Highway Safety reveals that only 32 states do so. Of those, only 15 require the permits to be held for a minimum length of time, usually no more than 90 days.

In other words, in the majority of states, there is no mandate that a young driver spend a reasonable amount of supervised time behind the wheel before attempting to obtain his or her license. Not surprising, almost all the states with the loosest licensing procedures have the highest crash rates for teens. Amazing to consider. All the more reason, then, to pursue a thorough instruction program of your own.

In addition, learner's permit or not, it's a good idea to obtain a driver's manual from your state department of motor vehicles. It should be studied even before you begin using the material in the next part of this book.

BEFORE THE VEHICLE IS MOVED

Teens typically are so anxious to begin driving that they don't want to learn much about the contraption they will be using in their newfound freedom. Girls especially are averse to learning the details. As the father of two daughters, I say this with authority. But it's important to know the basics about an automobile or whatever vehicle will be driven. So before the lessons begin, make sure your teen spends some time studying the machine.

No need to give an extensive course. For one thing, few of us possess such knowledge these days. Modern vehicles are very complex machines. Some of them have more onboard computer power than the Apollo spacecraft of the early '70s. Not much do-it-yourself maintenance is advisable anymore. Still, it's useful to give youngsters an understanding of what's under the hood, what does what and, especially, which components require periodic checking. This all may seem obvious to you, but to most teens, everything is strange and new. An introduction is in order.

In newer models, the owner-maintenance components are clearly marked: the oil dipstick, transmission fluid dipstick, brake and power steering reservoirs, radiator expansion tank and windshield washer fluid tank. Drive belts are also important and when broken can be a source of serious trouble. Take some time to go over the function of each of these components. If you need help, use your owner's manual.

Inspect the tires and, if you know how, demonstrate how to check the tire pressure (best done when the tires are cold).

With the hood still open, start the engine. Show the power plant at work to give a sense of the energy at the driver's command. Then turn the engine off and let the youngster sit in the driver's seat. Go over all of the vehicle's controls, from the gas and brake pedals (and clutch, if applicable) to the gearshift, lights, turn signals, wiper controls, ignition switch, heating and air conditioning controls, and so on. Again, if you need help, use the manual.

Also discuss the instruments. Pay particular attention to the three critical gauges (or warning lights). A warning from each requires a different response. The important ones monitor temperature, oil level and battery power. We'll discuss these later. For now, just point them out.

You also should discuss the fuel gauge. Most fuel gauges don't read truly. When the tank is full, the needle moves above the "F" mark. When the needle indicates halfway, the tank is usually only one-third full. And when most gauges read "empty," they are not quite empty — although it's still advisable to refuel well before the gauge hits bottom. Also, sometime early during the lessons, stop at a service station and demonstrate how to fuel up.

Don't forget to open the glove compartment and show the owner's registration card and owner's manual. The manual should be read and studied. It contains a lot of useful information, and this is a good time to begin learning about vehicle maintenance and care.

Last, let your teen turn the key and start the engine.

Today's vehicles have many different starting procedures, so you will have to fill in the specifics. Most modern ignition systems are electronic, so there's no need to depress the gas pedal while starting. Just turn the key all the way to the start position, wait until the engine catches, and release. Older models may need some help from the gas pedal.

The same goes for shutting the engine off. Sometimes a button must be depressed on the steering column before the key can be removed.

The main thing to teach is that once the engine starts and the key is released, the key should never be turned to the starting position again. If you ever have done this, you know why. The noise is pretty awful as the gears from the starter motor jam into the gears on the engine crankshaft.

You might even want to let your teen try a double start one time, just for the experience. It's usually enough to convince anyone not to do it again. But maybe not. In any event, practice the engine start several times, until the act becomes comfortable.

Be sure your teen understands where the gearshift position should be when the engine is started ("Park" on an automatic, and either neutral or first gear, with the clutch depressed, on a manual transmission). And make sure the parking brake is engaged before starting up.

A FEW WORDS ABOUT TEACHING

As you study the material in this book, and prepare to teach your teen, try to keep in mind that everyone learns best by doing. It's an approach based firmly on principles of human psychology and physiology. The mind and body can adapt to many conditions and activities. It's a survival mechanism. The key to successful adaptation is repeated exposure.

Driving, learned properly, is a process that becomes automatic, allowing the mind to relax without sacrificing attention. But the only way it can be learned properly is by repetition. This isn't to say that you shouldn't spend time talking about what to do. It's just that for some people, there may be a temptation to overdo it.

One of the things I discovered during my years as a teacher was that certain methods can get in the way of the learning process. For example, many people have a tendency to teach by asking open-ended questions or posing "fill in the blank" situations:

"What should you never do if you're approaching the crest of a hill?"

Or, "The most important thing to do after you start the en-

26

gine is _____."

Or, they simply spend too much time lecturing about proper technique.

Try to avoid these methods. They really aren't effective ways to teach. For one thing, they tend to create a tension between you and your student driver. People naturally are put on edge by them. In your own experience, haven't you felt uneasy, being on the receiving end of such questions?

Instead, briefly and in a very straightforward way, tell your teen exactly what you want him or her to know, and explain the reason for it. Ask once in a while if he or she understands everything you've discussed so far. Otherwise, keep things moving. Let the student perform the lessons.

As you proceed, try to include as much real-time instruction as possible. Calmly and matter-of-factly, comment on the performance as it happens. Also — and this is very important — act as your teen's co-pilot. Keep your own attention well ahead — and behind — on the road. There will be many situations and hazards your youngster will not be able to anticipate until he or she is more experienced:

— Developing congestion ahead, for example.

— Vehicles that may emerge from blind entranceways or parking spaces.

— Certain impatient drivers who you know will be lane-weaving around you.

— And potholes. Young drivers seem particularly oblivious to potholes. Potholes should be avoided or encountered as slowly as possible.

There won't be a shortage of road hazards. So you must serve double duty, as instructor and co-pilot. You'll find that the co-pilot role will be very valuable. It is the best way to impart knowledge, judgment and experience. By narrating road conditions and pointing out potential hazards, you will help your teen develop and strengthen his or her own sense of awareness.

If something isn't being done correctly, say so, as soon as

you notice it. But do it gently. Mistakes are part of the process, so there's no need to become emotional. You have to expect them. Be calm and review what happened immediately.

Speaking of which, as mentioned earlier, it's a good idea to spend a little time at the end of each session reviewing everything that was covered and anything unexpected that happened. Do it while everything remains fresh in both your minds. Remember: Brief/Perform/Debrief. If your teen is experiencing a particular or persistent problem, note it in the lesson log for future reference.

Regarding the lessons, I designed them to increase the level of complexity gradually. Each step should be repeated enough so that the student driver recognizes the proper procedures and begins making his or her own corrections. It is important to stick with each step until the student can perform all of its components well and consistently. If not, *it's a risk to move on to a more complicated situation.*

Remember to be just as quick to praise good performance as you are in pointing out mistakes. Be encouraging. It's a way to build a young driver's confidence, and to keep a strong bond between you.

If you are old enough to have a child of driving age, you have amassed your own body of experience on the road. Try to make use of it whenever you can. If you disagree with one of my recommendations, replace it with your own. Or present both sides and explain why you think your way is better.

I am convinced that the methods described in this book will provide a very solid basic level of skills for your teen. But they are by no means the only ways to do things. Everybody's experiences are different. You have valuable knowlege of your own. Use it. This process should not be about the book teaching your child. The book is a starting place. The process should be about you teaching your child.

THE BEST PLACE TO START

Okay, the preliminaries are over. The learner's permit has been acquired. It's time to let the student take control of the vehicle.

Where should you start?

The best place is a big, unoccupied parking lot. There are plenty of them around:

— an office building after hours

— a shopping mall early in the morning

— your local place of worship any weekday

— your high school parking lot

A high school lot may be doubly useful because it may contain painted lanes and pylons for driving instruction. Look around. You'll find a suitable place. Try to find one that has several rows of spaces, so you can drive in continuous patterns.

Empty parking lots are ideal because they offer plenty of space as well as defined areas. They are very forgiving of errors. The one I chose was in a nearby neighborhood park. It was perfect: two paved areas split by a grassy median and connected at both ends. It even had speed bumps, which also can be useful. Most important, although the lot was relatively small, it was almost always empty during weekdays after school. Find an empty parking lot, and you'll be ready to begin the instruction.

THE FIRST DAY

Drive to your designated practice lot and pull into a parking space. Try to use a space with either a concrete stop or a curb at the end, so there is a visual reference. Put the gearshift in "park" (or neutral, if a manual transmission) and engage the parking brake. Turn the engine off. Switch seats, then...

Stop for just a moment and look at your child. Accept that he or she is not a child anymore. A new relationship between you is about to begin.

Before the vehicle is started again, your teen needs to learn what must eventually become an important habit:

THE PRE-DRIVE CHECKLIST

You should go over this list from now on, every time you begin a lesson, until the student driver performs all the actions without prompting.

— *Fasten the seatbelt.* If the vehicle has an automatic shoulder belt, the lap belt should be adjusted as well. Make sure you are belted also.

— *Adjust the seat.* It should allow the driver's foot to rest comfortably on the gas pedal without stretching. But it needs to be far enough away so the foot can be moved quickly from the gas to the brake — again, without stretching.

It's important for the driver to be at least 10 inches away from the wheel if the vehicle is equipped with an airbag.

If the seat has other adjustments, such as height, make sure it is elevated enough to allow good visibility over the steering wheel and all around. A common mistake among many drivers is to keep the seat too low.

If the seat back can be adjusted, make sure it isn't tilted back-ward too much. That can cause strain to the neck and arm muscles over time.

— *Adjust the mirrors.* All the mirrors should be properly positioned to give the widest possible field of vision behind the vehicle. The center mirror should give an equal view to the right and left behind.

The side mirrors should show just a slight view of the edge of the vehicle. This is important because the vehicle edge provides a frame of reference for other vehicles and objects. On the other hand, if too much of the vehicle shows in the mirror, the driver's field of vision is probably too narrow. That's dangerous, because it will widen the blind spots.

Blind spots are gaps in vision, whether straight ahead or via the mirrors. If they are large enough, other vehicles can occupy blind spots and the driver won't see them. That's why mirrors should be used to help see behind and to the side, but they should not be relied upon entirely.

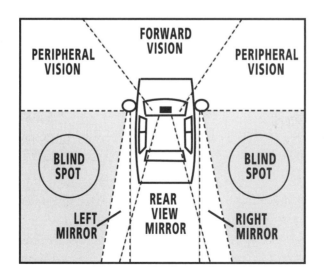

— *Adjust the head restraint.* The back of the driver's head should hit it in the center and should not have to travel more than a couple of inches before making contact.

— *Adjust the steering wheel,* if possible, so it's comfortable. The best position is tilting slightly away from the vertical. And the wheel should be far enough away from the body that when gripped it draws the elbows away from the chest.

— *Lock all the doors.* This adds a measure of security. Some vehicles even have automatic locks that engage as soon as they start moving forward. Locked doors are less likely to spring open in a crash, and they can prevent intruders — infrequent but real threats in today's society — from getting in.

GETTING A GRIP

The hand position on the steering wheel has become even more important since the introduction of airbags. Most experts recommend the "nine o'clock/three o'clock" position, to keep the hands away from the airbag in case it inflates during a crash. It permits the rapid and easy movement of the wheel.

I also recommend either "ten o'clock/four o'clock," or "eight o'clock/two o'clock," depending on which feels more comfortable. Neither one would interfere with the deployment of an airbag, and both offer plenty of control and flexibility, especially if the hands are extended far enough away from the body.

The position to stay away from — in terms of both control and airbag safety — is with one or both hands at the top of the wheel. That's common among drivers, but it interferes with effective vehicle control, and it invites injury if the airbag deploys.

As mentioned, the lessons in this book include the development of five main themes. That is, five approaches to driving that underlie everything else there is to learn.

Four more will be covered later. The first of the five is: **CLEAR THE WAY.**

It means never move the vehicle anywhere until you look first. You must constantly "clear" the way ahead or behind by looking. And you must stop or slow down whenever your ability to see where you're going is restricted. *This should be practiced from the very beginning and never forgotten.*

When you pull out of a parking space, make sure there is nothing immediately in front of or behind the vehicle. This should be done by looking around before you get in. No big deal. Just make a quick mental note. Are there any small children or pets nearby? If so, might they wander in your path — particularly if you're backing up — while you're getting ready to move? Are there toys or bicycles or shopping carts in the way? You want to clear an imaginary zone around the vehicle. The same applies as long as you are driving. When you start out, make a quick scan in all directions to be sure you're clear.

Whenever you arrive at a stop sign or an intersection, keep looking in every direction where there may be approaching traffic until the way is clear. As all drivers soon learn, it only takes a second or two of inattention to produce an unwanted surprise.

We'll discuss this theme frequently as we go through the lessons. But for now, concentrate on the idea: CLEAR THE WAY.

CLEAN AND CLEAR

Speaking of clear, it's very important to keep your windshield clean. The same goes for side and rear windows. This sounds extremely simple, but as you will quickly see in your driving sessions, it's something that can be very annoying if not taken care of. It even can be dangerous.

Substances continually are accumulating on your windshield. Dirt, road grime, tree sap, insect carcasses, leaves, pollen and bird droppings are common contributors. It doesn't take long before the glass becomes dirty. So it's a good idea, _every_ time you start out, to check the windshield. If it's a little dirty, use your washer and wipers to clean it. If there is anything major obstructing your view, take the time to clean it off before you start out.

It's also a good idea to clean all your windows every time you refuel the vehicle. Most service stations now provide a tuffy sponge and squeegee at the self-service pump. Use them. The main thing is to get used to keeping your windshield and windows clean.

TEN STEPS TO BASIC SKILLS

Back in the 1950s, the National Aeronautics and Space Administration developed a program to train astronauts. The key component of the approach was conditioning. Scientists and technicians developed tests and exercises that were designed to simulate as closely as possible the experiences and sensations the astronauts would encounter on their missions.

The more experiences that could be simulated, the more confident and successful the astronauts would be. Their fears could be "adapted out," as the designers of the training program often said.

That was the theory. For a while, it could only be a theory, because nobody actually had been up into space. Nevertheless, the scientists did their best to simulate their best guesses, and much of their work was validated by the reality of the missions.

The same approach can be applied to driving, which is an endeavor that at first can seem unnerving and possibly even frightening to someone with no experience. It also can be dangerous if a novice driver is confronted with a situation for which he or she is unprepared. It just isn't possible for a teenager, no matter how bright and coordinated, to jump into a car and instantly display skill and assurance. There are too many decisions to be made, and correct decisions about driving cannot be made through intuition.

Good driving behavior is based on experience. That's why it is very important to take sufficient time to teach your teen to drive. He or she must adapt to all the sensations of being behind the wheel, in most of the situations likely to be encountered. And those situations must be encountered gradually.

In this section, we'll go through ten separate steps. Each one is more complex than the last. The idea is to begin slowly and simply, and gradually move into more challenging conditions. For many teens, the early stuff may seem too simple. It isn't. It's fundamental. The early lessons will provide the foundation for the more complex tasks. Don't neglect them.

It never is necessary to complete all the material in a step in one day. In fact, it's inadvisable. Cover as much as seems comfortable within the time of the lesson. Then either start over the next day and go farther into the material, or begin where you left off. The point is to make sure you don't stop practicing a lesson until the student has mastered all of it. This is particularly true in the later stages, where the instruction takes place in real highway traffic.

Don't put your teen in a situation that you don't believe he or she can handle. It's dangerous to do so.

STEP ONE:
BASIC MOVES

This lesson takes place in the empty parking lot and covers the most basic movement and steering of the vehicle.

Each session in Step One should begin with the student driver repeating all the points we discussed in the previous section:

— fastening the seatbelt

— adjusting the seat and head restraint

— adjusting the mirrors

— adjusting the steering wheel

— locking the doors

— checking or cleaning the windshield

— mentally clearing the zone around the vehicle

Why bother, you might ask. After all, you're only going to be inching around an empty parking lot. But remember, you're trying to foster good habits here, so proper rehearsal should take place every time your teen gets behind the wheel.

Pretty soon, it will become automatic. Sitting behind the wheel will become a common experience and will include certain very specific sensations of adjustment and comfort: position of the mirrors, angle of the back, distance to the steering wheel, and so on. At that point, if something doesn't feel right, the young driver will correct it. For now, the task is getting accustomed to sitting properly in the driver's seat, and it should involve making sure everything is in its proper place — including the driver.

TEENS   PATIENCE, PATIENCE

If all is ready, we can begin. For today, and the next few days, we're just going to move the vehicle slowly around the lot.

And I mean, s-l-o-w-l-y! The speed should be hardly more than the vehicle moves on its own.

Turn the engine on.

With the foot on the brake pedal, release the parking brake and move the gearshift into reverse.

But don't move yet. Just hold the vehicle still, in gear, engine running, foot on the brake.

It's a new experience, so get used to the feel of it for a moment.

Then, after a quick look on both sides (remember, CLEAR THE WAY), slide your left hand to the top of the wheel, drape your right arm across the top of the seat, turn and look out the back window.

If anyone is nearby, don't move. Wait until the immediate area is completely clear. Likewise, during Step One, anytime a vehicle or pedestrian approaches, stop the vehicle. You don't want to interact with anything just yet.

All clear? Good. Very gently, ease up on the brake pedal. Allow the vehicle to move backward about 20 feet, so it is completely out of the space. Then just as gently, depress the brake and stop.

You should be looking through the back window the whole time, not using your rearview mirror. You don't want to try any turns right away. The backing up position is too new for that. Now, face forward, shift from reverse into drive (or first gear) and move the vehicle back into the parking space. Try to match the front end with the curb or the edge of the pavement.

It might seem strange, backing up the vehicle for your first move. But one of the most important things to learn at first is where your vehicle's extremities are — its front and back corners. You need to gain a sense of the space the vehicle occupies before you can move it around and into tight places.

By starting with a small reverse move, you learn how much of the vehicle is behind you. When you pull back into the space, you begin to learn where the front end is.

| PARENTS | POSITIONING THE VEHICLE

Make sure the teen pulls all the way into the space. The idea is to develop a sense of where the front of the vehicle is. When the maneuver is completed, have the teen put the transmission back into park (or neutral), put the parking brake on and shut off the engine. Then, have him or her get out and look where the front end is in relation to the end of the space.

If the vehicle was placed properly on the first try, fine. But repeat the drill anyway, several times. If the teen is having a little trouble, take more time to repeat the drill, over and over if necessary, until the vehicle can be stopped consistently at the end of the parking space.

AROUND AND AROUND

Next, begin moving around the lot. Have the teen back out of the space and straight across the traffic lane into the facing space. No turning while backing up just yet. Then have him or her pull back into the traffic lane, turning one way or the other, but signalling before the turn. Begin circling around the lot. The signal should be used every time there is a turn, just for practice. Emphasize steady motion and staying within lane markers.

TEENS   STEERING

When you approach a turn, move one hand or the other to the top of the wheel, depending on the direction (left turn: right hand up, and vice versa), then go hand over hand at the top of the wheel until the turn is completed.

Move your hands back to driving position and let the wheel slip gently through your fingers as the vehicle straightens out. But don't twist your wrist and grab the wheel palm-up to turn. It's an awkward position that limits how fast you can turn.

One tip: don't look at your hands or the wheel. Look where you want to go. Your hands will automatically steer the vehicle in that direction.

PARENTS   KEEP IT SLOW

The vehicle shouldn't be traveling more than ten miles an hour, just a little above idling speed, for the duration of Step One. Once in a while, have the teen stop in the lane, then start up again. Work on stopping and starting smoothly, easing on and off the brake, pressing gently on the gas.

Next, have him or her try pulling into a parking space from the lane. Be sure to signal first. Don't offer help the first time, but note how well the vehicle is placed within the lane markers. No need to step outside again. Just open the doors and look down. The vehicle should be in the center of the space and parallel to the lines.

When you back out this time, back out while turning into the lane. Start again with the left hand at the top of the wheel, and keep that hand on the wheel while turning. It's true that using two hands gives more control, but keeping the right hand on the wheel prevents your body from turning around far enough to see completely behind you. It restricts your vision. When you move very slowly, you need vision more than two hands. And you can stop immediately if necessary.

Here are the two keys to backing out well (aside from keeping alert so you don't bump into anything):

1. End each turn with your front wheels pointed in the general direction of your *next* move. (Back out to the left? End up turning your wheel to the *right*.)

2. If you can possibly avoid it, don't turn the wheel when the car isn't moving. It puts a strain on the steering components and can wear them out over time. And it greatly increases tire wear — just like rubbing an eraser.

Begin circling the parking lot again and after a while, try backing into a space:

1. Pull past the space slightly and turn away from it. Remember that before you stop, you must turn the wheels toward the next direction you want to go.

2. Back the vehicle into the space. Look out the rear window, and use the rear of the vehicle to guide you into proper position. Straighten the wheels before you stop.

It may take a few tries, but soon you'll get the hang of it. You might want to get out after the first time, to see where the rear of the vehicle ended up. It should line up with the back of the space, not hang over onto the sidewalk or grass.

ALL TOGETHER

The drill now is to practice all the components of Step One — starting and stopping smoothly, staying within traffic lanes, turning, pulling into and backing out of parking spaces. And remember the pre-drive checklist every time a lesson begins.

All this should be done, of course, in an empty lot. Continue the exercises until the teen can complete all of them with some precision — but not perfectly. Don't overdo things at this early stage.

PRACTICE "CALLED STOPS"

As you go through repetitions of Step One, every so often, say "Stop." Whenever you do, no matter what's going on, the student should bring the vehicle to a complete stop immediately. Not a panic stop, however. You don't want the tires to screech. Just a firm, smooth stop. No questions asked. No warnings. Immediate stop. The idea is to get the teen accustomed to moving quickly from the gas pedal to the brake.

Mention ahead of time that you are going to do this. Explain what you expect him or her to do, and why.

The called stop is your safety net. Use it regularly until you get into real traffic situations. Practice it at unexpected times until the teen reacts to it quickly and reliably. Then it will be available for emergencies. The teen will be conditioned to hearing it and will react properly.

ABOUT THE CLUTCH

Fewer and fewer vehicles have manual transmissions these days, so it's likely you're teaching your teen with an automatic. A stick shift adds complexity to the process, but not unacceptably so. In some ways, it's preferable to learn to drive with a stick. Just like riding a bicycle, once learned, it's never forgotten.

There are two very basic rules to employ with the clutch:

1. Ease out the clutch? Press—gently—on the gas. Push in the clutch? Ease off the gas. No matter how often you engage the clutch or change gears, stick to the rules. You may even want to exercise your feet for a while until you get the hang of it.

2. After you shift, take your foot off the clutch. Don't rest on it. Even slight constant pressure can wear it out.

As you engage the clutch, add fuel to the engine. But do it gradually. Just a slight pressure on the gas pedal is enough to prevent the bucking and stalling that is common among novices trying to master the stick shift. In fact, if you're in first gear and on a level surface, you don't need the gas at all. Ease the clutch out gently all the way and away you'll go.

In the parking lot, it's unlikely you'll need to go into second gear. The purpose of Step One is basic movement. We'll save shifting for Step Two.

STEP TWO:
PARENTS   BACK ROADS, QUIET STREETS

After a few trips to the parking lot, it's time to take to the road. Find the least-traveled nearby group of side streets or roads available. In that vicinity try to find a parking lot that is occupied but not busy. You're going to want to keep to a very low speed (for a standard transmission, no higher than second gear), so you don't want to interfere with or impede other drivers.

There are plenty of suitable streets and roads in most neighborhoods. If not, you may have to do some scouting. The idea is to find an area to practice where there is very light residential traffic. You don't want to use a thoroughfare because you don't want to encounter any "thru traffic" — cars passing through areas.

People tend to be a lot more patient if you're crawling around a neighborhood. They can see you've got a novice driver and they're likely to give you leeway. Not so on the traffic arteries. There, short tempers are common. A slow-moving vehicle can be viewed as an invasion of territory. Stay away for now.

If the teen can drive directly to your destination without encountering traffic, let him or her do so. If not, you drive. Find a quiet place to park, then switch seats. Again, start each session with the pre-drive checklist.

TEENS   KEEP IT SLOW (STILL)

Remember to check in all directions before you move the vehicle. Then move out, slowly, no more than about 15 miles an hour the first time, and keep it under 25 for the duration of Step Two.

What you want is to begin to gain a comfortable feeling with the vehicle moving just a little faster than before, on a street instead of the parking lot. You want to move steadily and stop smoothly. Don't jam on the brake. Push in the pedal. For a really smooth stop, ease up on the pedal slightly just before the vehicle stops moving.

Don't be impatient. Take it easy at first. Master the control of the vehicle before you try for speed.

PARENTS   SECOND GEAR

Begin to get your teen used to shifting gears. For now, stay with first and second, even though the engine may rev a little high. Now first gear should be used only for starting out. He or she should shift into second as soon as the vehicle is moving.

A SHIFTING TIP

Never downshift into first gear when the vehicle is moving. It puts too much of a strain on the engine and transmission. When you come to a stop, stay in gear until you've almost slowed down completely. Then push in the clutch. Get into the habit of shifting back into first gear as soon as you've stopped moving. That way, you always will be ready to start out again.

PARENTS   ON QUIET STREETS

Continue using the called stop, but be sure no other traffic is around when you do. As your teen begins to explore quiet streets, the first real driving encounters will occur, although not too frequently. Probable encounters will include:
— stop signs
— oncoming vehicles
—occupied parking lots (but don't try parallel parking yet)

TEENS   STOP SIGNS

Don't just pull up to a stop sign. Its placement is a very inexact process. If there's a crosswalk, stop in front of it. If not, pull up to the end of the street or road, until you can see in all directions.

But keep your eyes ahead until you stop. If the view at the corner is blocked, watch out for pedestrians or cyclists moving into the crosswalk, especially from the right.

Many drivers, when they make right turns, tend to pull well into an intersection while looking left. If the view happens to be blocked on the right side, and they're looking left while driving right, they could miss someone and run right over them.

Signal if your intention is to turn. Then stop — completely. Stop means stop. Look in all directions, then pull out. Remember to CLEAR THE WAY.

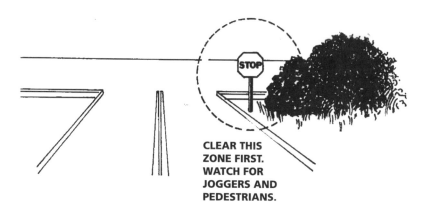

CLEAR THIS ZONE FIRST. WATCH FOR JOGGERS AND PEDESTRIANS.

FIRST MEETINGS

If you're using side streets and back roads, they are likely to be narrow. So oncoming traffic can be intimidating at first. The tendency of a beginning driver is to look at an oncoming vehicle. Don't. It tends to make you steer toward it.

For close encounters, keep your eyes mostly on the lane ahead. Concentrate on the empty space. But also pay some attention to the near front corner of the oncoming vehicle. It will provide an edge, and the earliest warning that you don't have enough room to pass.

When in doubt, slow down or stop and let the other traffic pass. At this stage, it won't hurt to interrupt things if necessary.

When you pull into parking spaces where the adjoining spaces are occupied, your vehicle should be far enough out from the space so you can turn into it easily. If

45

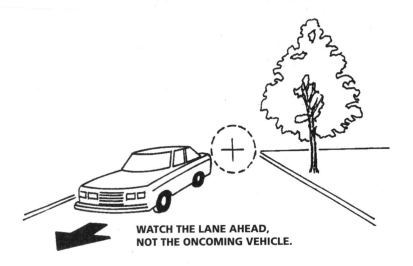

**WATCH THE LANE AHEAD,
NOT THE ONCOMING VEHICLE.**

you have enough room, you should be able to pull straight in, leaving more or less equal space on both sides.

Most of the time, however, you will have to steer into the space. If so, the leading corner of your vehicle should stay close to the adjoining vehicle on the outside of the turn. Follow along the side of that vehicle until you're about two-thirds of the way into the space. Then turn toward the center of the space and straighten out the wheels.

Do this very slowly and carefully, so there's no danger of scraping or bumping another vehicle. When in doubt, stop, back out (after you CLEAR THE WAY behind you) and try it again.

| PARENTS | PARKING DRILLS |

Have your teen practice pulling into spaces between other vehicles at least a dozen times. Have him or her back out in different directions. When you think the time is right, have the teen try to back into a space, using the same technique as in the empty parking lot. This should be done slowly, as the teen looks through the back window and guides the back end of the vehicle into the space.

Continue these drills until the teen moves easily into and out of the parking spaces and along the quiet streets or roads. Things to watch: getting used to the steering wheel and the pedals, moving the vehicle in a straight line down the road, stopping precisely, and executing simple interactions with other vehicles.

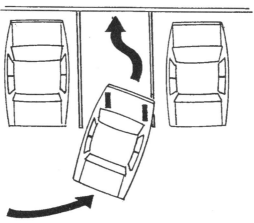

**STEER CLOSE TO THE VEHICLE
ON THE OUTSIDE OF THE TURN.**

TURNAROUNDS

Find a dead-end, two-lane street — a cul de sac — to begin practicing turnarounds. This used to be an important part of the behind-the-wheel portion of the license exam. Some states still may require it. It's not a major maneuver. But the teen should be able to handle the vehicle in tight spaces.

The vehicle should be turned around without backing up more than once and without bumping any curbs. Practice turnarounds several times at least, until they can be executed easily.

<u>Note</u>: Don't try this anywhere but on a dead-end street. Turnarounds are illegal in most jurisdictions.

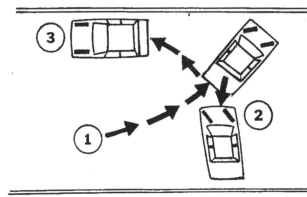

A TURNAROUND IN THREE MOVES

`TEENS`   TIGHT TURNAROUNDS

These are easy maneuvers because they are performed at very low speed. Just remember three things:

1. Don't turn the steering wheel unless the vehicle is moving.

2. Always end each maneuver with the front wheels turned in the next direction you want to go.

3. Move slowly.

Start the turn as far to the right side of the roadway as possible. Turn sharply left, moving to the edge of the road. Straighten the wheel and then turn right just before you stop. Keep the front wheels from hitting the curb.

Back up with the wheels turned hard right. Then straighten out and turn left before you stop. Keep the rear wheels from hitting the curb.

If you've done it correctly, you should be able to pull away on your third move.

`PARENTS`   A LITTLE FASTER, A LITTLE BUSIER

Next find an area that is a mixture of neighborhood streets and minor traffic routes — but no four-lane highways. No road should have a speed limit higher than 35, and during Step Two the vehicle speed should be kept to 30 or under (third gear, sometimes, on a stick shift).

An ideal situation is a string of different neighborhoods that can be reached by crossing over, or driving briefly along, secondary two-lane routes. Maybe there's a traffic light or two in the area. That's fine. But you don't want too much traffic yet.

The chief new ingredient here is more frequent encounters with other vehicles, pedestrians and possibly animals.

You won't need to use the called stop as frequently — maybe once in a while, if necessary, just to keep it available as an option. Once or twice, though, you may have to use it for real.

As the two of you drive through these areas, begin to discuss the possible hazards that can arise:

— Pedestrians. Is there plenty of room to allow them to cross safely ahead? Or, if they're walking along the road, is there enough room to go around them?

— Children playing in a yard. Are they playing with a ball that could roll into the street? Are they chasing one another, so one of them could run in front of the vehicle?

— Animals near the road. Are they in a position to dash in front of the vehicle suddenly? Is there only one, or could there be two or more, unseen?

— Hedges and walls. Could they conceal vehicles about to pull out of driveways?

— Occupants of parked vehicles on the side of the road. Are they about to open their door? Is there enough room to avoid them if they do so?

— Approaching the top of a hill. Is there a vehicle stopped on the other side? Is someone standing in the middle of the road? Can the vehicle be stopped in time to avoid a hazard?

— Likewise, going around a blind curve in the road. What could be around the corner?

Whenever you encounter a situation that might be hazardous, you should react in the same way: proceed with caution. How?

As soon as you notice something, the first thing to do is take your foot off the gas pedal. Ease up your speed. This is very important. You should do this anytime there's a possible obstruction or hazard ahead. Almost every good driving maneuver begins with this action.

Keep your eyes on the object or area of concern. If it gets closer — and if there is no easy way to steer clear — move your foot to the brake and press gently. Begin to slow down.

If there is no other choice, stop the vehicle.

For example, if you're approaching the top of a hill and your view of the road is shortened, ease up. Keep looking over the top. Then, if something does appear suddenly, you'll have time to deal with it. If the road is clear, you can steer around. If it isn't, you can stop. Either way, by looking and easing up, you have preserved your options.

If children in a yard begin moving toward the road in front of you, ease up in case you have to stop. Be aware of them until you pass by. If there's the slightest chance they will move in your path, stop. Don't risk tragedy.

If a pet or other animal — like a squirrel — is in a position to dash under the vehicle, ease up. Animals can be unpredictable. Watch them.

Here's a tip about encountering animals near the road: Most animals cannot deal with vehicles. Even dogs and cats can make wrong moves. Animals' natural defenses aren't prepared for a massive body that moves rapidly in a straight line. It baffles them. That's why so many end up under the wheels of vehicles.

When you approach an animal near the road, take your foot off the gas. If the animal doesn't move out of your way, slow down and tap your horn quickly once or twice, but not too loudly. You might scare it into shock. A couple of quick beeps will send most critters scampering away from the noise.

| PARENTS | DEALING WITH IMPATIENCE

It's unlikely that another vehicle will tailgate you in this environment. But these days, anything is possible. If someone does, find the earliest place to pull over, have your teen signal and do so.

During Step Two, you want your teen to slow down at the first sight of a possible hazard. You want to help him or her to develop sensitivity. A good way to do this is through exaggeration — slow down for everything.

Later on, when the teen is more experienced, he or she will detect things more quickly and automatically, and know when to ignore and when to react. But for now, anything remotely hazardous should require slowing down. So you don't want anybody following you closely.

STEP THREE:
BUSY BUT SLOW ENCOUNTERS

A good location to introduce your teen to busy vehicular and pedestrian traffic is a shopping center parking lot. The reason is that while the place may be busy, the speeds are low.

Find a lot that's suitable and, if necessary, drive your teen there. Spend at least several sessions cruising the lanes and continuing to practice pulling into and out of parking spaces.

There won't be much new in the way of driving skills here.

The purpose of Step Three is to get your teen into the habit of noticing everything that's going on in the immediate area — to become sensitive to hazards in crowded places. It's something that will be very valuable later on, when real traffic encounters begin.

As you move around the lot, point out anything that could become a hazard. Do it in real time, so the teen can get into the habit of spotting potential problems. Every time something causes concern, suggest a way to deal with it.

Eventually, the teen should call out hazards as well. You want to keep repeating these sessions until he or she can pick things out nearly as quickly as you.

After a while, stop prompting. Have the teen call out everything. When an entire session can be completed without something being overlooked — and with everything receiving a proper reaction, it will be time to move on.

One caution: just because the speeds are low, don't assume this is a safe environment. Shopping center parking lots are a major source of fender-benders because there is so much simultaneous activity, and because the rules aren't as clearly defined as on the road. You must watch pedestrians and other drivers closely.

TEENS   LOW-SPEED HAZARDS

Even though you're driving slowly in a parking lot, there's plenty that can go wrong:

— A car can pull out suddenly in front of you, either from a space or a crossing lane.

— A child or adult can dart out from between two cars into your vehicle's path.

— If you're backing out of a parking space, you could back into a person or another vehicle.

— A vehicle or person could appear suddenly from around a corner.

Sharpen your skills by keeping an eye on everything around you as you drive. The key to doing it safely is to keep your speed low and be ready to react to anything that might happen.

DON'T ASSUME ANYTHING

If, for example, you are about to drive past someone who is stopped and waiting to pull out, but isn't looking at you, don't assume he or she will look before moving. Your best reaction: foot off the gas.

Keep your eyes on the other party until you are seen.

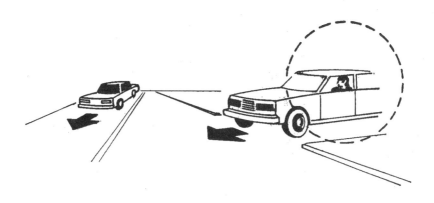

If you are approaching a vehicle that is ready to back out of a space (How can you tell? If the back-up lights are on, the transmission is in reverse) don't assume the driver will wait for you to pass. Again, best reaction: foot off the gas. If you see any movement at all, stop.

__Your horn is a last resort. Never use it unless you must warn someone that they are about to bump you. Don't use it as a way to express disapproval. It's rude and it makes people angry. Reserve it as a warning device only. And tap it. Don't hold on it.__

OUTSIDE, THEN INSIDE

Before you take your teen to the streets, try one more variation on the busy parking lot: a busy parking _garage_. A parking
garage offers new challenges because the lanes tend to be nar-
rower and the spaces tend to be smaller. The entrance and exit
ramps also are narrow. And garages require driving with the low-
beam headlights on.

Just remember that low-speed places aren't necessarily safe
places. Careless and unskilled drivers are everywhere.

Have your teen practice the same techniques in the garage
that were employed in the parking lot. Continue to move along
the lanes and pull into and out of—and back into—spaces. Make
sure everything is done slowly and carefully.

Since this is a new environment, resume the hazard-spotting.
When he or she can maneuver through the garage easily and call
out all potential problems, you can move on.

But first...

A parking garage is a good place to begin talking about personal safety. Sometime in the coming months, your teen will obtain his or her license and will begin driving alone. That includes,
sooner or later, entering a parking garage. You need to talk about
choosing a parking space sensibly, such as avoiding isolation and
dark corners and scanning the garage for suspicious characters.

_If your teen is a daughter, it means, especially, avoiding
what many police departments say is a favorite tool for individuals with sexual assault on their minds: vans with darkened or
covered windows. Since you can't see inside these vehicles, they
can conceal someone waiting to spring out._

TEENS PARKING GARAGE ALERT

**If you are a female, never park next to a van with
darkened windows. If one is parked next to you, never try**

to enter your vehicle on that side. Enter on the opposite side or, better still, as a precaution, wait until there are other people around before you approach your vehicle. This may sound overly cautious, but it is a situation that is real and related to many assaults on young women.

As a general rule, always try to park in plain view of a busy entrance or pedestrian walkway. Your best situation in a parking garage is with people and in the light. The worst is isolation and darkness.

| PARENTS | TAP THE WALL

A parking garage is also a good place to begin to instill a little respect in your teen for the power and energy contained in a vehicle. You can do this by performing a small and — if done properly — harmless experiment.

Find a parking space that abuts a concrete wall or barrier. Have the student pull into it and stop, then move forward until the front bumper comes in contact with the wall. Not very fast, just enough to feel the shock of the impact. I guarantee you there will be a shock. Even a one-mile-an-hour impact will send a shiver through both of you.

Make sure it's a solid concrete wall, by the way. Don't use a wall that's made of concrete blocks, which are hollow and which could be damaged by even a slight bump from a vehicle.

It's just a little reminder of how powerful the forces are that involve moving a ton and a half or more of motor vehicle.

If you have any doubts about this idea, or are worried about damage, you drive. Tap the wall at the slowest possible speed. Then do it a little more forcefully until you get a sense of what feels right. It really doesn't take much velocity. But it will leave an imprint on your teen — as a driver or as a passenger.

STEP FOUR:
STOP AND GO

Once your teen gets used to dealing with the slow traffic and commotion of shopping center parking lots and garages, you can move on to busy but low-speed traffic in commercial strip areas, where there are frequent stop lights and lots of cars entering and exiting the road.

Low speed is a key factor here. Keep it down but increase the interaction, so the teen can stop quickly if something goes wrong. Use roads and streets that have speed limits of 35 or under. Also, given the increased level of complexity, Step Four should only be attempted in daytime and in good weather.

The traffic will be an important new challenge, and your teen will be experiencing several new situations:

— moving onto, off, and along commercial strip routes
— stopping and starting at traffic lights
— making right and left turns
— changing lanes
— avoiding lane blindness ("the canyon")

There is much to learn, and so Step Four should take considerably more time to complete than any of the first three steps. I recommend a minimum of five sessions before moving on.

At first, map out a course for your teen that involves turning onto and off of a four-lane commercial route. Follow it for several miles. Be sure your teen stays in the right lane and drives at or near the (low) speed limit. Find a suitable (right) turnoff, like a side street. Turn onto it, find a turnaround, then reverse your course.

Whenever approaching a turnoff, make sure he or she signals in plenty of time, slows down gradually, and turns smoothly out of the traffic. Do this repeatedly for a couple of hours. It's a way of giving your teen just a taste of driving in traffic.

This drill should encompass the following situations:

— turning smoothly into lanes and maintaining a steady position within a lane

— maintaining a steady speed within traffic

— maintaining proper distance behind vehicles and giving plenty of warning when turning or stopping

— using the rearview mirrors to keep track of traffic behind

— reacting quickly and properly when traffic lights turn yellow (come to a stop unless you are _within_ two seconds of crossing the intersection)

— paying attention so he or she doesn't hold up traffic when the light turns green

— coming to a full stop, watching for cross traffic, and turning right on red

— watching out for red light runners

— avoiding pulling abruptly ahead when the side view is blocked by larger vehicles, such as trucks and vans

Make sure the teen faces everything on the list and handles each one well. All the while, continue to practice hazard-spotting, like you did in Step Three. Same rules: when the teen spots everything and handles every situation properly, move on.

TEENS DEALING WITH TRAFFIC

The drill here is to combine two skills: scanning for hazards and reacting to them, and blending in with traffic in a steady and predictable way.

You can do this by extending your attention as far ahead and behind as possible.

CLEAR THE WAY.

How? If you spend too much time and effort trying to identify hazards, won't it make you nervous? Won't it become very tiring?

Not if you do it properly.

First, look well ahead of your vehicle. Don't focus on the pavement, or on the vehicle in front of you. Instead,

try to maintain a relaxed, general gaze forward.

Don't stare. Let your eyes move around naturally. Glance at the rearview mirrors frequently. But keep your main attention in front of you.

Second, don't press it. Try to relax. You're developing the ability to use your peripheral vision as your early warning system. Use it to create an imaginary CLEAR ZONE that extends in all directions from your vehicle.

You won't be able to do this right away. It will take some time before it happens automatically. But you must practice it every time you drive, so that it becomes a habit.

MAKING A CLEAR ZONE

Peripheral vision is the most effective tool you have to protect yourself. It is also the least tiring way because it uses the natural abilities of your body. Just like many other animals, we humans have the ability to recognize inconsistencies in our environment. Those inconsistencies instantly attract our attention.

Inconsistencies? Yes, such as something that moves. Or something that is different from its surroundings. Something that contrasts, either lighter or darker.

Animals, especially predators, are extremely well adapted to detect movement. Something that moves across their field of vision instantly arouses their attention. Then they focus on that object until they determine what it is. You can make use of this same ability while driving. When you are moving along the road, whether in traffic or alone, the road and the landscape take on a consistent and predictable pattern. The pavement passes beneath your vehicle in a certain way. So do the sidewalks, streetlamps and road signs. And if you drive properly, you blend into the flow of traffic. Everyone moves along at basically the same speed. It's a moving CLEAR ZONE.

Within the zone, everything is fine. You are relaxed. It's only when something changes that you snap to a higher level of attention:

— Someone changes lanes in front of you,

— or signals to turn,

— or applies the brakes.

— Someone pulls out in front of you from the right,

— or pulls out from the left into the lane beside you.

Any actions like these may require an immediate re-action from you. So you have to notice what's happening immediately. Then, most times, you only need to: ease off the gas. The same with anything that happens along the side of the road, or on the pavement itself:

— A pedestrian waits to cross the street.

— A vehicle waits to pull out of a parking lot or a side street.

— A bicyclist rides along the right side of the lane.

— A pothole appears in the lane ahead.

All these things represent inconsistencies with the normal pattern of traffic, pavement, or scenery. In a sense, they've invaded the CLEAR ZONE. As soon as they appear, they should attract your attention. As you approach them, or they approach you, keep your attention on them, so you can react as quickly as possible if you need to.

The most important thing is to notice potential hazards quickly. The sooner you recognize them, the more time you'll have to react if necessary. Why is this so important? Because it takes time and distance to bring a vehicle to a stop. If you don't have enough time or distance, and you have no room to steer out of the way, you're going to hit something.

This is very simple but very important. Lack of time to react is the first component of a crash. Consider this:

If you're traveling at 35 miles an hour, you'll need at

least 100 feet to stop. That's one-third the length of a football field. The reason is that at 35 miles an hour, you're traveling at about 50 feet per second. That's right, every second means 50 feet.

By the time you notice something, recognize what it is, move your foot to the brake, apply pressure to the brake, and brake the vehicle to a stop, at least two seconds have passed. Two seconds is as fast as anyone can stop in that situation. And two seconds at 35 miles an hour means 100 feet. That's the absolute minimum distance you will need. The faster you go, the more distance you'll need. That's why you've got to keep your attention well ahead.

By the way, if someone pulls or merges into an adjoining lane, what's the quickest way to tell if they're moving into your lane?

By watching their front wheel. If it's turned properly, it's not headed into your CLEAR ZONE, so the vehicle is no hazard.

DON'T VIOLATE YOUR OWN CLEAR ZONE

Remember, it's always possible to get into trouble by failing to spot an obstruction. A typical situation can happen at a stop sign or stop light in a line of vehicles waiting to make right turns. The problem occurs when someone ahead of you is waiting to turn. If you look left at oncoming traffic and forget to check whether the vehicle in front of you has actually pulled away — BAM! Many fender-benders have resulted from this situation. So if you're looking left and the road is clear, don't forget about what's directly in front of you. CLEAR THE WAY.

Another problem, that we'll discuss later, involves allowing your CLEAR ZONE to become too small, so that you can't stop or react in time if a hazard enters it. Not

only must you CLEAR THE WAY, but you must do so far enough ahead to keep out of trouble.

| PARENTS | ALONG THE STRIP

Make at least several passes back and forth along the strip during each lesson. Try to do it when there is moderate but not heavy traffic. The teen should stay in the right lane. No major interaction yet, just getting used to the sensory input by rolling along a somewhat busy thoroughfare.

Watch out, however, for drivers pulling out suddenly from side streets and parking lots, and for drivers who take too much time turning off the roadway. Make sure your teen learns to anticipate these mistakes in other drivers.

Continue to be the co-pilot and keep up the hazard-spotting as long as necessary. Also watch the line the teen maintains. That is, he or she should be following the contours of the road in a smooth way. No weaving within the lane.

The same with speed. Steady and consistent. Gradual starts and stops. No acting like a jackrabbit. And no screeching to a halt.

TEENS STOP LIGHT? DRIVE LIGHT

When a traffic light turns red ahead, ease off the gas and coast to the stop. No need to burn excess gas just to go nowhere. Many drivers — young and old — tend to hold their speed until the last possible moment when they approach a stop sign or light. Some people actually try to pass other vehicles before they get to a stop. This is wasteful and sometimes dangerous.

When the traffic light is already red, ease up. Hurry-up-and-wait is a useless activity. And remember to ease off the brake pedal just before your vehicle stops.

WATCH OUT FOR LIGHT RUNNERS

One common hazard at controlled intersections is drivers who fail to stop for red lights. It's a growing problem, so you can't just move out as soon as your light turns green. You could move into the intersection and be broadsided by a red light runner.

So when you're stopped at an intersection and the light turns green, CLEAR THE WAY. Check both directions before starting out.

INCREASE THE COMPLEXITY

When your teen reaches a good confidence and skill level with this exercise, begin to incorporate more complicated maneuvers:

— Turning right into a parking lot. Find a space and pull in, then pull back out and return to the strip, turning right onto it.

— Changing lanes and making a left turn, first at a traffic light with a left turn arrow, next at a light without a left arrow, and last at an entrance to something without a light. Left turns should be practiced turning first behind and then in front of oncoming traffic — _if_ there is enough time and distance to do so.

— Returning to the strip and making a left turn onto it.

These exercises will require a lot more skill and judgment, so be careful. If your teen is having any kind of trouble adjusting to the new challenges, back off a little. Return to the maneuvers he or she was performing well for a while. Attempt the more complex stuff a little later.

Remember, this process is about adapting gradually to new situations and building good habits. Every young driver progresses at his or her own rate. There's always a little nervousness at each new situation, but you have to judge whether the student is getting in a little over his or her head.

If there's any doubt, take extra time. Too much time spent at any of these stages is much better than too little. Make sure your teen performs each new skill well before moving on.

TEENS   CHANGING LANES

Changing lanes is relatively easy. It can be done with only a slight turn of the wheel. A lane change should not be abrupt. But it shouldn't take too long, either. Just a smooth slide over to the left.

Make sure no one is about to stop suddenly in front of you. Put your signal on and check the rearview mirrors — inside and driver's side. If everything seems clear...

Don't move just yet!

Many accidents occur in just such a situation. The reason is that there are blind spots in your mirrors, especially if they are positioned properly. People glance at the mirrors, assume it's safe to change lanes, and — well, you know. So hold your lane for just a moment, turn your head and *quickly* look at the next lane.

CLEAR THE WAY.

If it's clear, move over, smoothly, turn signal off.

Do it every time you change lanes. The same with moving to the right:

— Turn your signal on.

— Check the rearview mirrors.

— Glance to the right.

All clear? Change lanes.

LEFT TURNS

Begin to try left turns at controlled intersections, first with left turn lanes and arrows and then without them. You should be in the proper lane well before it's time to turn.

As you approach the intersection, put your turn signal

on at least five seconds before you reach the place to turn. Do this even if you're in a "Left Turn Only" lane. You need to be perfectly predictable.

Sometimes streets are designed to permit two lanes at a time to turn left. If so, it's important that you maintain your lane all the way through the turn. You don't want to drift into someone.

This is another situation where looking ahead will serve you well. As you turn, keep looking ahead to where you want to go. Pay particular attention to the inside part of the lane. But don't move toward the inside of the curve while you turn. Stay in the center of the lane.

| PARENTS | TURN WITH CAUTION

Turning left in front of oncoming traffic can be tricky. In fact, it can be more than tricky. It can be dangerous. Your teen needs to be able to judge speed and distance with accuracy. The first few times, provide close guidance. He or she must develop a sense of when to move.

At this early stage of building skills, traffic should be at least ten seconds away before the student attempts to move across the path. Don't cut it close. Allow plenty of time. If there's any doubt, wait. Later on, the lead time can be cut down to about five seconds.

Also important when turning: have the teen keep the wheel straight until beginning the turn. If you are sitting with your wheels turned to the left, and someone hits you from behind, you could be pushed into oncoming traffic.

| TEENS | LOOK FOR THE SPACE

When you need to turn left _behind_ oncoming traffic, focus your attention on the space behind that traffic.

64

Don't look at an oncoming vehicle. Drive into the empty space behind it.

LOOK TO THE SPACE
BEHIND ONCOMING
TRAFFIC.

By the way, a good guideline for making left turns in front of traffic is what I call the Three-Second Rule. That is, after you complete your turn — meaning you are completely out of the way of oncoming traffic — if it takes at least three seconds for that traffic to cross in your rearview mirror, you turned in plenty of time.

AVOID 'THE CANYON'

When you are driving along in traffic, a hazard can develop that has nothing to do with the roadside or the pavement. I call it "the canyon." It happens any time your sideways vision is blocked because there is a larger vehicle, like a truck or a bus, beside you — maybe even on both sides.

This situation can be hazardous even when you are stopped, or when you are approaching a cross street. You have to be careful not to jump out suddenly because there may be a vehicle — such as a red light runner — or a pedestrian about to cross in front of you. The drivers in the bigger vehicles can see. You can't.

Do one of two things here:

— Wait until the other vehicles start moving. Roll along side them until you're through the intersection, then lag behind or move ahead.

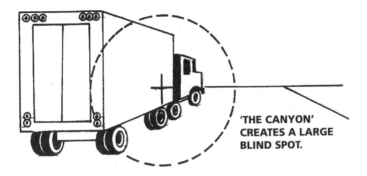

'THE CANYON'
CREATES A LARGE
BLIND SPOT.

— If you are trying to make a right turn, and the left lane is obstructed, move out very slowly until you can see that no traffic or pedestrians are approaching.

Avoiding "the canyon" is just one more variation of **CLEAR THE WAY.**

PARENTS   LOCATION, LOCATION

It may seem so simple as to be obvious, but don't assume your teen doesn't need a little help learning how to find places along streets and roads, or figuring out the best routes to get somewhere.

When I was teaching one of my daughters, I told her one day to drive to a shopping center located about three miles from our house. I was shocked when she asked me how to get there.

"Why? We've been going there for years," I said.

"That's true," she replied, "but you always drove, so I never paid attention to how we got there."

It wouldn't hurt, in this and future steps, to have your teen practice following directions and finding street addresses as part of the lessons. Many localities now have detailed roadmaps available, so you can study the map and discuss your route ahead of time.

You can also explain your hometown's system of street numbers and street names. This can be a big help as your youngster begins traveling to new places.

STEP FIVE:
COUNTRYSIDE

In the previous step, you introduced your teen to the bustling and frequently nerve-wracking environment of traffic. Most of the challenge involved interacting with and avoiding other vehicles at relatively low speeds.

Now we're going to spend some time working on pure driving skills, getting used to the road and the terrain, the vehicle itself, and all the physical motions that driving requires. It should be a more pleasant experience than the shopping strip: less traffic, more scenery. Just don't let your guard down. There are plenty of hazards in the countryside, too.

You'll want to find an area that is sparsely populated and not well-traveled. Find some lengthy two-lane roads that wind through the landscape but aren't main arteries. Lots of curves and hills are desirable. The top speed for this drill is 45.

This will involve all the gears on a stick shift except overdrive, and downshifting will be practiced.

The co-piloting and hazard-spotting should continue, except most of it should involve the road and the landscape. Passing is not yet advised, unless it's absolutely necessary. And stick with good weather and daylight.

As long as there are no major highways or arteries, your teen can drive to the area you have selected. You will be teaching about highways later. For now, he or she is completely inexperienced and doesn't belong in traffic at highway speeds.

In Step Five, we will work on these specific skills:

— following the contour of the road

— strengthening peripheral vision

— adjusting speed as necessary for curves and hills (alternating between the gas and the brake, and the clutch, if necessary)

— identifying new potential hazards

— reading and understanding road signs

DRIVING IS SENSING

The process of driving is about three-fourths sensory and one-fourth logical. It's like sports. Most of it is automatic. The higher brain functions don't govern. You don't think your way along the road:

"I want to turn right. I'd better move the wheel in that direction. Yes, that's far enough. Now I need to straighten out."

Instead, your eyes recognize the path that your brain wants to follow. Without thinking consciously or deliberately, your brain orders your hands to turn the wheel along that path. It orders your feet to press on the gas or the brake so the speed of the vehicle is proper for the condition of the road.

Thinking comes in when you reach a fork in the road and decide which one to take. Or when you begin to feel tired and decide it's time to stop for a break. Or, most frequently, when a hazard presents itself in the distance and you decide how to deal with it.

But when something happens very quickly, you must react reflexively. The habits and skills must be well-developed to protect you. They won't become well-developed unless you take the proper amount of time.

So don't assume that because you're now moving onto roadways that you're ready for anything. You're not. Be patient. You have a long way to go.

PARENTS   TAKE THE TIME

Spending at least ten sessions driving through the countryside, an hour or so each time, will help the teen's mind and body become more accustomed to this process. Basically, it's a hand-eye coordination drill.

In order to follow the contour of the road as smoothly as possible, you need to keep your eyes well ahead of the vehicle. If you look ahead, you will tend to steer a very smooth course in the center of the lane. If you shorten your focus, you will begin weaving.

You are driving at a higher speed now, so your stopping distance will be increased. At about 45 miles an hour, you will need at least 130 feet to stop. So you should be looking at least 130 feet ahead at all times.

When you're driving through the countryside, however, there will be times when you are unable to see that far. Around a blind curve, for example. Or over the top of a hill. It stands to reason, then, if you can't see 130 feet ahead, and if it would take you at least 130 feet to stop, your CLEAR ZONE has disappeared. You are in an unsafe situation.

Any time your visibility decreases, slow down. If you only can see 100 feet ahead, you should be doing no more than 35. If you're down to 50 feet, it's 25, and so on. Whatever the situation, always reduce speed until your CLEAR ZONE matches or exceeds your speed. _**This is the most important rule you can follow.**_

CHECK YOUR SPEED

By the way, how do you know how fast you're going? Look at your speedometer once in a while — but just for an instant. If you look away from the road, you are driving blind for the duration of that look. At 45 miles an hour, a one-second look translates into 66 feet of blind travel. So keep your glances very short, and only when the road ahead is completely clear.

Take extra care with your teen on curves and hilltops. Not only is visibility restricted, but inertia will begin to affect the vehicle. This can be very frightening to someone who hasn't experienced it before. It can lead to sudden loss of control.

Having control involves learning how much speed is prudent on a particular curve in the road. Different speeds can be attempted safely, depending on visibility, pavement conditions, and stability of the vehicle. Young drivers don't know this yet. And it's very difficult to teach, because it involves an acute sense of the limits of the vehicle in a given set of circumstances. That sense must be developed over time. It is the product of experience.

Until that sense is acquired, it's usually best for you to make the proper judgments. When you believe it's necessary, get the student to slow down to the proper speed, and work on the habit of slowing down whenever he or she feels uncomfortable in a situation.

Theme Two of Five:
TEENS   LEARN THE LIMITS

Curves can be very tricky, because physical forces act on the vehicle. Forces like inertia and gravity.

When you begin turning the wheel, the momentum of the vehicle is still headed in a straight line. Gravity holds the vehicle to the ground, the tires grip the road, but the inertia causes the vehicle to lean away from the turn.

Inertia also causes you and everyone in the vehicle to be pulled to one side or another during the turn.

It can sound very technical, but basically you need to know that the faster you try to go around a turn, the more powerful inertia becomes. Gravity and friction remain the same. Therefore, at some point, inertia becomes too strong and you don't make the turn. You fly off the road.

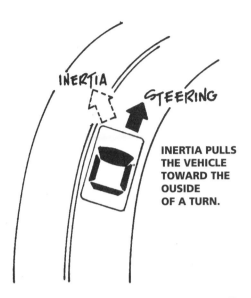

INERTIA

STEERING

**INERTIA PULLS
THE VEHICLE
TOWARD THE
OUSIDE
OF A TURN.**

How can you know all this? Well, you can't, not right away. It takes time to LEARN THE LIMITS, which is the second of our five themes. Until then, you can only keep safe by being cautious. Approach curves and turns at a comfortable speed. As you gain experience, you will learn more about what a vehicle can and cannot do under certain conditions.

In order to complete a turn safely, inertia must either be reduced or overcome. Most of overcoming it is accomplished by the friction between the road surface and the tire treads. Part of it also involves the strength of the vehicle's structure, which keeps it from falling apart because the wheels are pulling it one way and inertia is pulling it another.

If the vehicle has a low center of gravity, it can make a very tight turn at high speed without flipping over. With a high center of gravity, such as can be found in many four-wheel drive vehicles, there is a greater chance of turning over. Likewise, if there is plenty of friction between the tires and the road, the vehicle will hold the turn. If not, you lose control and slide off the road.

71

Several road conditions can cause tires to lose "traction," as it is called:

— water, from rainfall or flooding
— dirt or gravel
— wet leaves
— ice and snow
— oil or other viscous fluids

If you encounter any of these unexpectedly on a curve, you'll slide right off if you're not prepared. Road friction is no longer strong enough to overcome inertia.

But remember, I said that inertia could also be _reduced_ as well as overcome. The best way to reduce inertia is to slow down.

And the best time to slow down is _before_ you enter the curve.

The same can be true sometimes at the tops of hills, although limited visibility is a much more frequent problem.

Still, it's important to remember that same forces that can cause you to lose control on curves can also operate on hilltops. On some country roads, taking a sharp hilltop too fast actually can cause the vehicle to lift off the surface of the road.

Yes, just like in the movies. Except that once the tires lose contact, there is no control at all. You are at the mercy of what is waiting on the other side. _Don't ever do this! It is extremely stupid!_

A few years ago, two teens were joyriding in a pickup truck one morning over a section of very hilly road near where I live. They jumped one hilltop and landed on top of a station wagon that was stopped behind a school bus. They killed two small children in the car and seriously injured the mother who was driving.

They caused a tragedy and ruined their own lives because they didn't CLEAR THE WAY and they didn't

72

LEARN THE LIMITS.

When you learn the limits, you will know what the vehicle safely can and cannot do under certain conditions. You will know how fast you can take a turn when the pavement is dry, wet or icy.

How can you learn the limits?

Practice, practice, practice.

And more practice.

Until then, you can't know. So the smartest thing to do is slow down before you become involved in a situation you can't control. And things can get out of control very, very quickly.

There's another reason to slow down before you enter a curve: unless your vehicle is equipped with an antilock braking system (ABS), braking on a curve reduces control even more.

One of the most common errors that young drivers make is to take a turn too fast, panic, and hit the brakes. Very often, this causes the vehicle to skid.

As long as the wheels are turning, the tire treads can transfer much of the energy from the vehicle's momentum to the road. But when you apply brakes, especially in a panic stop, the treads lose much of that ability, and so they simply slide across the pavement.

On a left curve, it means sliding off the road. On a right curve, it means sliding into oncoming traffic. You don't have to be traveling very fast for this to happen, either, if the turn is sharp enough. Say you start to take a turn and you quickly realize you're moving too fast. What do you do?

Do not hit the brakes.

First thing: foot off the gas.

Second thing: _tap_ the brake pedal several times, but ride out the turn. (With ABS, keep constant pressure.)

Even with ABS, it's advisable to go into a turn at the proper speed. It lowers the chances of something going wrong.

COUNTRY HAZARDS

As your teen cruises over the countryside, he or she will encounter new potential hazards that you will need to point out:

— oncoming traffic (again, not too much of this, but it's a new situation because the vehicles are traveling faster)

— tractors and farm machinery on the road or crossing it

— large animals, such as deer

— hidden driveways

— cross-country cyclists

— pedestrians

— railroad crossings

Each of these requires a slightly different response.

COUNTRY CRUISING

You will be using your hands and feet a lot in these drills. Moving over country roads requires frequent changes in speed and direction. It's the best way to sharpen your abilities to steer, brake, shift gears and, especially, spot hazards.

You will know you're doing well in this situation if your speed changes and turns are smooth and gradual. If so, you are reacting properly to everything on the road.

There will be more of this later, but for now, concentrate on two things:

1. Steer very smoothly to follow the contour of the road.

2. Work your right foot back and forth easily from the gas to the brake.

You are taking a turn properly if you can maintain a

steady speed through it and if you don't have to correct your steering. Keep looking well ahead through turns, concentrating on the inside of the curve because it gives you the earliest sign of a hazard.

Regarding the gas and the brake, there are four movements to choose from:

1. Foot off the gas (the most frequent move).
2. Move to the brake.
3. Ease on the brake.
4. Full press on the brake.

On a smooth, straight highway, you might not need to use any of these movements for long periods. But on a curving, hilly country road, your foot will be moving almost constantly.

How do you decide what to do? It's just like steering: you look where you want to go and your hands follow. Here, concentrate on your CLEAR ZONE and your foot will follow. You want to be able to stop or steer clear if you need to. Therefore you must adjust your vehicle's speed to the situation.

Foot off the gas is a precaution — just in case. Foot to the brake means you're ready to stop. Whether you use the other two moves depends on what happens in front of you.

Can you think about all this? No. You must practice it until you develop a good sense of what to do. Then, you can do it all the time without thinking.

Practice, practice, practice...and more practice.

FREQUENT SHIFTING

This is another skill that will require lots of practice to develop. For now, concentrate mostly on steering and braking. You don't need to learn all the nuances of downshifting yet. Just follow three simple rules:

1. Slow down first, then shift.
2. Slow down a little, shift down a little.
3. Slow down a lot, shift down a lot.

Foot off the gas and use your brakes to slow down. _Then_ change gears. Use lower gears for consistent engine power, not to slow down. When you decelerate for curves or hills, you're also slowing down the engine's revolutions. So it's a good idea to drop into third gear to give the engine enough leverage to maintain adequate power.

If you have to slow way down, under 20, for example, you should drop into second gear for the same reason.

ONCOMING

On a two-lane road, oncoming traffic might seem a little more intimidating to you at the speeds you are now traveling. You should be cautious. Even at 35 miles an hour, two vehicles approach each other at a combined speed of 70. Even with the best seat belts and airbags, a head-on collision at that velocity can be extremely dangerous.

At 45 miles an hour each, the combined speed is 90.

What's the CLEAR ZONE at 90? Nearly 300 feet, the length of a football field. So it's important to maintain a steady course within your lane. No need to move to the right as an oncoming vehicle approaches. Just hold your position. As it passes, keep looking down the road beyond it. But notice its near edge. Again, that edge provides the earliest indication it may be too close to you.

BEWARE DROP-OFFS

There's a dangerous situation that can develop almost instantly when you're driving along a country road, especially during your learning months. It's called a drop-off, and if you respond to it the wrong way it can be deadly.

A drop-off occurs when your front wheel suddenly leaves the pavement and drops onto the shoulder, which is lower than the road. It happens because you have taken a curve too quickly. Or, you somehow have allowed the vehicle to drift off the pavement. Whatever the cause, a drop-off is noisy and disturbing.

It can become dangerous if you obey your first instinct, which is to turn the wheel sharply. Don't. It can cause the vehicle to whip sideways and cross into the oncoming lane.

Instead, remember that piece of advice I've been repeating all along: At the first sign of trouble, foot off the gas. Do not hit the brakes. Then, move the vehicle a little further to the right.

That's right — move right. You want to get the right front wheel away from the edge of the pavement, where it might jerk suddenly to the left and force you back across the road.

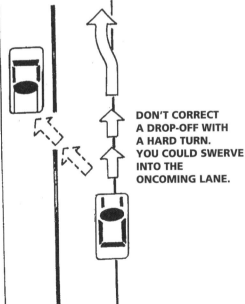

DON'T CORRECT A DROP-OFF WITH A HARD TURN. YOU COULD SWERVE INTO THE ONCOMING LANE.

Keep the front wheels parallel to the road until you slow down. Then gradually steer the vehicle back onto the pavement.

This is important, so let's go over it again:

— At the first sign of a drop-off, foot off the gas.

— Avoid hitting the brakes.

— Move a little further to the right, away from the edge of the pavement.

— Steer parallel to the road until you slow down.

— Gently ease the right wheels back onto the pavement.

The critical thing is not to panic. It will make for a bumpy ride, but if you handle it correctly, a drop-off will be temporary and a minor inconvenience.

PARENTS   IT'S WORTH PRACTICING

The danger of an overreaction to a drop-off is so great that it's a good idea to practice it a few times. Remember, experience is the best teacher. But it only should be attempted on a road that is guaranteed to be empty. Here's what you need:

1. A stretch where the shoulder drops a couple of inches off the pavement

2. Good visibility so there is no chance of traffic — either following or oncoming — appearing unexpectedly

3. Familiarity with the recovery procedure

At low speed, have your teen move the vehicle off the road, then recover. Do this several times, gradually increasing the speed, until the student can perform it smoothly at about 35 miles an hour. Just watch out for traffic.

TEENS   OTHER COUNTRY HAZARDS

If a tractor is crossing the road, the most important thing is to spot it in time. If you're practicing maintaining a

CLEAR ZONE in front of you, there should be no problem.

If the machine is moving in front of you, chances are it's moving very slowly. The CLEAR ZONE should detect it in time. Slow down gradually behind it. Wait until the road ahead is completely clear, then accelerate smoothly and pass.

Deer and other large animals near the road can be unpredictable. Never assume they won't jump in front of you. Slow down until you can stop in time if you need to, and then ease past them. Remember to use short bursts of your horn to drive animals away.

In areas where deer are common, there will be deer crossing signs posted. This really should not affect your driving if you are maintaining a CLEAR ZONE in front of you. Any time your visibility is restricted, slow down until it returns.

Hidden driveways are a constant possibility in rural areas. But the CLEAR ZONE also should take care of them. If a driveway is hidden, it means overall visibility is reduced, which means your CLEAR ZONE is reduced. You should slow down until it expands again.

Theme Three of Five:
SHARE THE ROAD

Countryside cruising is a good place to learn the third of five themes. It's very simple. Use common courtesy wherever and whenever you can. Give others a break — cyclists, for example.

Cyclists usually travel on the right edge of the lane but not the shoulder of the road. Whenever you see them, SHARE THE ROAD.

Ease up as you pass them, and pass them only if there's plenty of room. Don't crowd. Many roads have rough shoulders or drop-offs that could spill a cyclist.

**SHARE THE ROAD.
GIVE CYCLISTS AND
PEDESTRIANS ROOM.**

Move toward the left to increase the margin of safety. If you can't pass immediately, be patient. Cyclists are allowed on most two-lane roads.

The same with pedestrians. Ease up until you pass them, move left to give them room, and don't pass unless it's safe. We'll talk more about SHARE THE ROAD later. It's an essential part of good driving.

THE SPECIAL DANGER OF RAILROAD CROSSINGS

Railroad crossings require special attention. A surprising number of motorists are killed every year because they don't take rail crossings seriously. Or, they mistakenly assume that a train can stop before it hits them.

Never. Repeat — NEVER — cross a railroad track unless you can see that it's clear, in all directions.

By clear, I mean at least a hundred yards - a football field.

What if you can't see a hundred yards? Stop the vehicle, roll down the window, and listen! If you hear a train approaching, but can't see it, stay put. If you can't see it, you can't tell how fast it's going.

If there is more than one track, and a train has passed, don't move unless you can see a hundred yards in both directions on both tracks. Again, if you can't see, listen until it's quiet.

Make no mistake. People die regularly at railroad

crossings. If you tangle with a train, you're going to lose. Don't take the chance.

By the way, always make sure the road is clear on the other side of the tracks. You never want to get stuck on the tracks. People have died that way, too.

| PARENTS | BEWARE OF TAILGATERS

Even though you and your teen are driving along roads with light traffic, sometimes vehicles may pull up behind you and follow closely. Get the teen into the habit of checking the rearview mirror regularly, at least several times each minute. If someone approaches closely from behind, take the first available turnoff. Keep the lessons concentrated as much as possible on curves and hills and roadside conditions.

Speaking of which, there are two things to emphasize every time your teen encounters a curve:

— Develop a keen sense of the arc of the curve, so that the vehicle remains in the center of the lane all the way through.

— Watch the inside edge of the roadside, which is the quickest way to detect sudden hazards.

If this is being done correctly, the vehicle will track smoothly in the center of the lane. If the teen's focus is too short, the vehicle will weave through the turn because corrections will have to be made.

TEENS LOOKING AND CURVING

As I keep mentioning, it's always best to look ahead while you're driving. But you don't want to look too far. If you gaze too far ahead, you could miss important details that are closer to you. Try to maintain your attention about five seconds down the road. For now, five seconds is plenty of time to recognize a hazard and react to it.

How do you tell what's five seconds ahead? Pick an object that you pass alongside the road. Count slowly to five and look in your rearview mirror to see how far away it is.

Now pick out something ahead that seems the same distance away. Count to five again. Pretty soon, you'll figure it out. If you keep practicing, after a while, you'll know instinctively the best distance to look ahead.

Don't stare at the same place on the road. Your eyes work best when they don't fix on the same thing for long periods. You have to keep looking _mostly_ far ahead, while glancing frequently at other things. If you encounter multiple curves, keep your attention on each curve's inside edge as far ahead as possible and you will steer the course correctly. When you see the curve ending, resume normal speed.

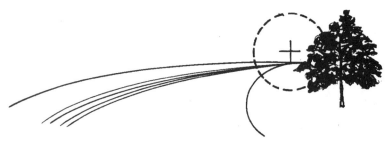

**ALWAYS FOCUS
ON THE INSIDE EDGE
OF A CURVE.**

Remember the following about curves:

— Slow down before you enter the curve.

— Look around the bend, concentrating on the inside edge.

— Stay in your lane all the way through the curve (on a curve to the left, don't cheat into the oncoming lane).

— Resume speed as you re-enter the straightaway.

ROAD SIGNS ARE FOR READING

When you are driving through the countryside, road signs take on added importance. They help you by identifying conditions and possible hazards that are beyond your range of vision. When you see a road sign, make sure you read it and understand it. Your state's driving manual should contain a section on road signs. Study it to make sure you recognize all of them.

PARENTS   ## TURNING ONTO ROADWAYS

One other important countryside exercise: pulling out from a stop sign onto a road, either right or left. It's a maneuver that requires caution and judgment, so make sure your teen practices it frequently and is very careful each time.

It's not hard to imagine what could go wrong in a situation like this, especially when visibility is limited. The key to safety is to keep looking.

TEENS   ## GET UP TO SPEED

When you have to pull out from a stop sign to the right, first CLEAR THE WAY to the right. Make sure nobody's about to walk or bike in front of you. *Then* look left and pull out if the lane is clear.

Make sure you accelerate smoothly until you reach cruising speed. Many people, when they pull out from a stop sign, have a tendency to think the maneuver is done as soon as they complete the turn. They poke along, taking too much time to get up to speed. In fact, it's a frequent experience to encounter drivers who do this without regard for oncoming traffic. They pull out and take their time getting up to speed, and thereby interfere with the flow of traffic. It's not a smart thing to do.

When you turn left, you have a more complex task, because you have to be aware of traffic approaching from both directions. You have to cross the near lane and enter the far lane. Traffic can approach very quickly, and on many rural roads, visibility may be limited. Even at 35 miles an hour, vehicles are closing on you at 50 feet per second. If you look left, turn and look right, and pull out, all within three seconds, something that wasn't within 150 feet before is now going to hit you.

Three things to remember when you pull out:

— Keep looking in both directions - left and right, left and right, left and right - until you have pulled out. **CLEAR THE WAY.**

— If one side has less visibility than the other, concentrate your scanning on that side, but don't neglect the other.

— As soon as you're in the lane, check your rearview mirror to see what traffic behind you is doing.

A SPECIAL NOTE ABOUT CENTER TURN LANES

Occasionally, you will encounter a road with a center turn lane. The center lane is used for left turns, but it's an uncertain place to be, because it can contain traffic traveling in opposite directions. The danger is that you will be in the lane, moving toward a left turn that is beyond an oncoming vehicle also in the lane. If neither driver is paying attention, you could have a head-on collision.

If you find yourself on a road with a center turn lane, and you need to make a left turn, don't cruise the center lane. Wait until you're almost at the turn. Signal, check _both_ your blind spot and the lane for traffic, and then move over, continuing to watch for oncoming traffic. You want to minimize your time in the center lane.

STEP SIX:

GETTING UP TO HIGHWAY SPEEDS

This is a variation of Step Five, except that it should take place — in this order — on uncrowded four-lane highways and on cross-country two-lane arteries. This is the time to introduce the student to highway speeds — within certain limits.

Top speed of these lessons is 55, which should remain the maximum for your teen during the entire first year of driving.

Even if you live in a rural area near an uncrowded interstate highway with a higher speed limit, don't allow your teen to drive faster than 55 the first year. Keep in mind that 55 translates into about 80 feet per second. Stopping distance — reaction time plus braking distance — is more than 200 feet.

That's a large CLEAR ZONE to maintain. It takes experience to do so. Despite all these drills and practices, novice drivers do not possess sufficient skills and judgment to go any faster _safely_. Impose a 55-mile-an-hour speed limit during the first year.

EASING ONTO HIGHWAYS

When you find an appropriate stretch of highway, have your teen spend at least several sessions cruising it, practicing all the same drills contained in Step Five. A clear stretch of four-lane highway shouldn't present many roadside hazards, so the teen can work on holding a good line and maintaining a steady speed.

Still, you will need to cover the following new situations :
— entering and exiting the highway
— merging with other vehicles
— passing other vehicles
— being passed by trucks
— emergency stopping and reentering highways

MERGING

Merging properly onto a highway can be a very tricky maneuver. It requires good judgment. It will test your youngster's ability. You want the teen to use the approach ramp and merge lane to accelerate until the vehicle is traveling at or near the same speed as the traffic already on the highway, then find an open space in the traffic and move into the lane. This is the correct procedure even if there's no traffic on the highway at that moment.

This is a very difficult maneuver when done in traffic. That's why you need to find a lightly-traveled road. Once you find a likely route, select a pair of exits that are only a few miles apart. Then just keep traveling back and forth between them, entering and exiting, over and over.

The goal at the entrance is first to observe and clear the ramp, accelerate smoothly up to the speed of the highway, then signal and merge into the lane. Remember, a lightly-traveled road allows room for errors.

You might want to wait on the shoulder until the ramp is empty. Trying to merge in traffic might make your teen timid about the maneuver. Use an empty ramp to build his or her confidence.

At an exit ramp, the turn signal should be on at least ten seconds before the exit. This should be done whether or not anybody else is on the road. You want it to become a habit.

It's also important to maintain speed until you move into the deceleration lane or the ramp itself. If possible, don't slow down until you are clear of the traffic lane.

TEENS   CLEAR THE RAMP FIRST

There are three keys to safe merging:

1. CLEAR THE WAY. Determine how much room there is ahead — on the ramp or the acceleration lane — before you have to move over.

2. Select your place in traffic ahead of time. That means you have to examine oncoming traffic, and judge its speed and distance, before moving onto the roadway.

3. Slip into traffic as close to the speed of the traffic as possible, not too fast or too slow.

Your place in traffic is like a moving target. It's a "merge slot," a large, imaginary space that is already moving with traffic at the proper speed. Once you identify it, maneuver the vehicle into it. Presto! You're now part of the traffic.

Look for the merge slot by looking to the side and glancing at your rearview mirrors. If the highway is empty, no problem. Pick out an imaginary space anyway, for practice.

But concentrate on the ramp ahead first. If you focus your attention on the highway or on oncoming traffic, you could ignore a hazard ahead of you on the ramp. Or the ramp might end suddenly, with no merge area. Usually, there is a road sign to tell you this, but not always. Whatever, it's critical that you CLEAR THE WAY on the ramp before moving onto the highway.

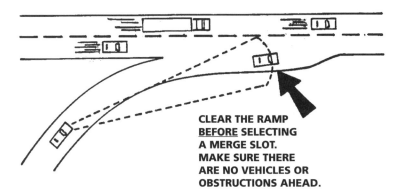

CLEAR THE RAMP
BEFORE SELECTING
A MERGE SLOT.
MAKE SURE THERE
ARE NO VEHICLES OR
OBSTRUCTIONS AHEAD.

Never stop on an entrance ramp, unless you have no choice. Why would you have no choice?

— There could be a stop sign or road construction.

— Somebody could have stopped ahead of you because they never found a merge slot.

Stopping on a ramp is _a very dangerous thing to do._ For one thing, somebody could come up from behind without looking and crash into you. For another, everybody that stops will have to wait until the highway is completely clear, because if they attempt to accelerate into traffic from a standing start, the other vehicles will have to move over or slow down to let them in.

The worst situation is when somebody attempts to merge from a stop ahead of an oncoming truck. They may misjudge the truck's ability to slow down or stop. Trucks require longer stopping distances than smaller vehicles.

By the way, in most states, traffic that is already on the highway has the right of way. You can't approach a highway and expect other vehicles to let you in. But if you merge properly, with steady acceleration, no abrupt swerves, no stomping on the gas or hitting the brakes, it should go smoothly. Give yourself as much room as possible, and glide into the lane. Signal until the merge is completed.

Even later on, when you attempt this in heavy traffic, you'll know it's been done correctly if it's done smoothly. This could be difficult for you for a while, so keep trying until you feel confident about it. You can't practice merging too much.

Just remember to CLEAR THE WAY. Pay attention to what's going on in front of you before you attempt to change lanes onto the highway.

EXITING

When you exit, signal your intention at least ten seconds ahead of time. If you don't know exactly where the exit is — it's on the other side of the crest of a hill, for example — begin signaling as soon as you see the exit sign or the ramp.

Be predictable. Signal to let drivers behind you know what you're going to do. When you reach the exit ramp, move over _before_ you slow down.

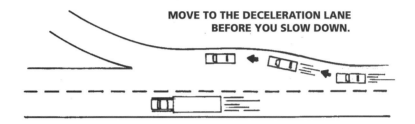

MOVE TO THE DECELERATION LANE
BEFORE YOU SLOW DOWN.

This is important: avoid slowing down on the highway. Slow down on the ramp. Many highway crashes are caused at entrances and exits. These are places where the speeds of vehicles can vary greatly. You can reduce your chances of a crash by joining and leaving highway traffic smoothly and at proper speed. Accelerate and decelerate on the ramps as much as possible.

LET 'EM IN

When the situation is reversed, and you are on the highway, encountering traffic that is entering and exiting, it is easier. The best thing to do is to be courteous and helpful to other drivers. SHARE THE ROAD. When you see a vehicle ahead on an entrance ramp, either move into the left lane if it's clear, or foot off the gas. Coast and wait for the vehicle to merge, then resume speed.

If the driver seems hesitant, flash your headlights quickly. If there's no response, or the driver appears indecisive, pass with caution.

Your best option is to move left. Next is to coast behind the vehicle. Last is to pass.

When a vehicle ahead signals to exit, coast until it moves over.

Your courtesy will go a long way toward allowing other drivers easy merges or exits. The roadway becomes a little safer because of your actions.

Be courteous, but don't depend on the courtesy of others. Appreciate good manners when they're displayed. But don't assume they will be offered. Take all the precautions you can to protect yourself. Make courtesy mandatory for you. Consider it a bonus from others on the road.

PARENTS   STAY RIGHT, STAY SAFE

A common mistake for drivers — both young and old — is to linger in the left lane. Don't allow your teen to fall into this habit. The left lane is supposed to be for passing or faster traffic.

You should know from experience that many drivers become angry and rude if someone ahead is blocking the left lane. They are likely to be just as impatient with a novice as anybody else. So keep to the right to stay out of their way.

TEENS   RIGHT ON

Even if the roadway is lightly traveled, get into the habit of staying in the right lane. Use the left lane only for passing.

If traffic is heavy (which shouldn't be the case until Step Nine), it will fill both lanes. Even then, stay to the right. Don't try to keep up with faster traffic at this stage of your development.

PASSING

Passing on a four-lane highway is relatively easy and safe, as long as you avoid being surprised by someone who's been driving in one of your blind spots.

As mentioned before, every vehicle has blind spots. They are spaces to the side and behind that aren't covered by the mirrors. Someone could be traveling near you in one of your blind spots at any time. The way to overcome this hazard is to CLEAR THE WAY. Check the mirrors and then look _quickly_ to the side to make sure no one is there.

As soon as you see a slower-moving vehicle ahead, clear the left lane. Signal and move over. Pass the slower vehicle, but don't pull back to the right just yet. Wait until you can see _both_ headlights of the vehicle in your rearview mirror (not the side mirror). Then signal and return to the right lane. You want to avoid crowding the other driver's CLEAR ZONE.

If the left lane isn't clear, continue to approach the slower vehicle until you're about three seconds behind it. For practice, you can tell this by taking any landmark, such as a roadsign, and counting the seconds from the moment the vehicle ahead passes it and the moment you do. Ease up and stay at that distance until the left lane is clear. Then signal, accelerate and pass. Again, pull back into the right lane only when you can see both headlights.

MORE ABOUT BLIND SPOTS

As much as you need to look out for other vehicles in your blind spots, try also to avoid sitting in someone else's blind spot.

How can you tell? If you can see the other driver in his or her side mirror, then he or she can see you. If you can't, the driver may not know you're there. Also, if you're travel-

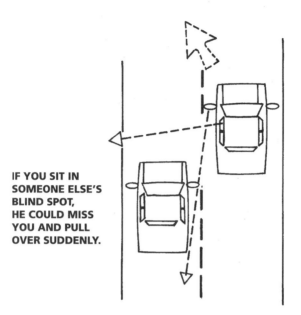

IF YOU SIT IN SOMEONE ELSE'S BLIND SPOT, HE COULD MISS YOU AND PULL OVER SUDDENLY.

ing at the same speed as a nearby vehicle and your front fender is beside their rear fender, either to the right or left, you are probably in a blind spot. Whenever this happens, try to move ahead or behind as soon as possible so you can be seen.

BEING PASSED

We'll cover being passed in traffic in Step Nine. For now, you need to know two things when trucks pass you:

— Be aware that big trucks create a "bow shock," a wide area of air turbulence around them. When they pass you, if they are moving five to ten miles an hour faster than you are, expect to feel a sudden push away from them. Hold your steering wheel firmly, and correct your heading if necessary.

— When the truck has passed you completely, and is two or three car lengths ahead, flash your headlights quickly several times. This is a universal "all clear" gesture. It lets truck drivers know that they are clear to move in front of you. It makes things easier for them. Most of them will say "thanks" by flashing their running lights.

It's another way for you to SHARE THE ROAD.

HOLDING THE LINE

When you're not merging, passing or being passed, work on maintaining a good line on the road. Stay in the middle of the lane and avoid weaving. You should know the best way to do this by now: keep your eyes several seconds ahead or, on curves, around the bend. But most times, avoid looking directly at the pavement in front of you. It creates too much visual activity and will tire your eyes quickly. Use your peripheral vision to scan the pavement for hazards.

After you've been driving a while, you will develop a sense of where your vehicle is in the lane. It will become instinctive. The best way to foster this sense is to keep your focus well ahead of where you are — at least a hundred yards.

Try also to maintain a steady speed. It will help a lot if you're calm and relaxed. The more you drive, the more you will develop a reliable sense of how fast you're going. For now, check your speedometer a couple of times each minute. Just glance down at it.

DON'T TAKE 55 LIGHTLY

In this time of increasing highway speed limits, and with so many drivers ignoring those limits, staying at 55 might seem downright pokey. Believe me, it isn't. When you drive 55, you are driving at the limit of your vehicle's ability to protect you in a crash — airbags or not. If you hit something at 55, your chances of survival are not good.

Don't take the speed lightly.

If you have any doubt about how fast you're really going, take just a moment sometime when you're doing 55 to observe a passing object, such as a bridge abutment or utility pole. Now try to imagine hitting it. All of a sudden, 55 isn't so slow, is it?

You can gain a false sense of confidence by looking at the open road. You might begin to think you're not moving very fast. In a word, don't. Your vehicle is carrying a tremendous of energy at that speed.

Think back about how that little tap in the parking garage felt, the one against the concrete wall at about one mile an hour. Think how an impact at 55 might feel. Never underestimate how serious highway speeds are.

| PARENTS | EMERGENCY STOPPING

While you're cruising a lightly-traveled highway, it's a good time to introduce your teen to the emergency stop. It can be an extremely important and useful maneuver, and it's relatively easy to learn because it's similar to handling a drop-off. Wait until the highway behind you is clear, then have the student practice. Try it several times during the highway lessons, whenever it won't interfere with other vehicles.

TEENS   STEADY, STEADY

An emergency stop done properly is like the combination of a drop-off and exiting. Except you're usually not lucky enough to do it on an exit ramp.

The key to a safe emergency stop is to slow down as gradually as possible and to give traffic behind you as much warning of your intentions as you can.

Here are the steps:

1. Foot off the gas (notice how many times this is the

best first thing to do?).

2. Turn your signal on.

3. Make sure the shoulder of the road ahead is well clear of obstacles.

4. Move over to the far edge of the pavement.

5. Continue coasting until your speed drops to about 45.

6. Gradually steer off the roadway and onto the shoulder.

7. Gently brake to a near stop.

8. Pull as far away from the road as possible, at least the width of a lane.

9. If you must remain near the roadway, turn your emergency flashers on.

It is very important to make this a gradual maneuver. Sudden swerves can throw the vehicle out of control. If you're driving a sport-utility vehicle, it could even roll over.

One possible reason for an emergency stop is a flat tire or a sudden loss of tire pressure, called a blow-out. The first time you ever experience this, it can be very unnerving. Your first impulse might be to slam on the brakes.

In a word: don't!

When one tire goes flat, it creates a severe drag on the other wheels. If you hit the brakes, you are adding to the instability of the situation. The best thing to do is to _steer_ your way off the highway. Hold a straight line and resist the temptation to brake. Bring the vehicle to a gentle stop using the steps listed above.

GETTING BACK ON THE ROAD

Make this maneuver as close to a merge as possible. First, judge how much room there is ahead on the shoulder before you return to the pavement. If there is plenty of room:

1. Turn your flashers off and your turn signal on.

2. Get rolling only if there is a break in traffic.

3. Stay on the shoulder until your speed is at least 45.

4. Move over as soon as possible — but don't swerve — and quickly accelerate to highway speed.

5. Turn your signal off.

If there is no room to make a rolling start, you will have to watch for a big traffic opening because you will have to do all your accelerating on the highway. Put your signal on and wait for a clearing. Keep watching your rearview mirror to see if someone behind you flashes their headlights or moves over to let you in. If they do, take advantage quickly.

**Spend as little time as possible on a highway if you can't maintain close to highway speed.**

Remember to be courteous to other drivers in this situation. If they're signaling an emergency stop, ease up until they're off the road. If they're trying to get back on the road, ease up and flash them in or move out of the lane if it's clear and pass them. SHARE THE ROAD.

| PARENTS | 55 ON TWO-LANE ROADS

When you think your teen has mastered the basics of merging, exiting, passing and being passed, and when you think he or she is holding good line and speed on that four-lane highway, it's time to move back to two-lane blacktop. Only this time, find one with a speed limit of 55. An old-fashioned cross-country artery, with a bit of traffic, both automobile and truck, some stoplights, side roads, driveways, curves and hills.

Now have your teen repeat all the drills in Step Five. Except remember that the CLEAR ZONE at 55 is at least 200 feet. There will be many circumstances along the road that won't provide such visibility. So there is likely to be a lot of variance in speed.

TEENS HIGHWAY SHIFTING

If you're using a manual transmission, you could be doing a lot of shifting. In general, it's advisable to keep the vehicle in the proper gear so you can accelerate easily without pushing the engine's revolutions too high.

If you have a tachometer, this is easy. However fast or slow you're going, the engine should be running between 1500 and 2500 rpm. That's a good range — 1500 for cruising, and 2500 or so for acceleration.

At the low end, try to keep the engine at a minimum of 1500 rpm whenever you're moving. A lower rate than that can strain an engine and rob it of all its power.

Without a tachometer, shifting becomes more challenging and intuitive. You need to begin to feel when the engine needs the help of a lower gear, and when upshifting is needed because it's revving too high.

PARENTS TWO SETS OF EYES ARE NEEDED

Your co-piloting will be very important here. Two-lane, 55-mile-an-hour roads are, mile for mile, the most dangerous highways in the country.

It's easy to understand why. When drivers pass, they must do so into the oncoming traffic lane. At 55, there's a combined speed of 110. When people behave impulsively or misjudge how much room they have, the results can be devastating.

High-speed head-ons have high fatality rates. So be extremely careful.

Work on the following new situations:

— pulling off and pulling onto high-speed two-lane highways

— encountering other vehicles pulling on and off

— following at a safe distance

— dealing with tailgaters

— being passed

Notice I didn't include passing here. That's because passing on a two-lane highway is too dangerous for learning drivers to attempt.

Let me repeat that:

Passing on a two-lane highway is too dangerous.

I'm not talking about passing a farm tractor or an ancient pickup truck that is puttering along at 25, although even those situations call for great care. No. It takes very strong skills and judgment to overtake another vehicle at 55 on two lanes with oncoming traffic. Save it for later, after the license has been obtained and the student has been driving for six months or more.

One more thing: I recommend using low-beam headlights at all times on roads like these.

TEENS ENTER WITH CAUTION

Pulling onto a high-speed two-lane highway requires even more caution than normal. Not only do you have to be sure there is no immediate oncoming traffic, you have to get up to speed quickly. Otherwise someone could be on your tail in no time.

Just like other tricky maneuvers, it will take some time to develop a good sense of when to move. It's best when you start out to "err on the side of caution," as they say.

Give yourself lots of room. If you have any doubts, wait. If there are others behind you and they seem to be growing impatient, wave them around you. Don't let yourself be pressured into taking risks.

But once you begin the maneuver, if you're out on the highway and in the lane, don't delay getting up to speed. That doesn't mean you need to "floor" the gas pedal. Just don't dawdle.

HIGHWAY TURNOFFS

Turning safely off a 55-mile-an-hour road with no exit ramps requires one critical ingredient: predictability. Signal at least ten seconds ahead again, with one extra caution: if there is traffic behind you, don't be tempted to use your brakes right away.

Instead:

— Put your signal on at least ten seconds ahead of the turn.

— Foot off the gas pedal.

— With a manual transmission, downshift one gear.

— Begin to brake gently.

— Slow down far enough to make the turn safely.

— Make the turn.

Remember to slow down _before_ you make the turn.

HIGHWAY ENCOUNTERS

If you're following the rules, encountering another vehicle pulling out or turning off should not be a problem. If someone ahead is pulling out, first thing to do is take your foot off the gas. Coast until they reach cruising speed. SHARE THE ROAD. With a manual transmission, if your speed drops much, downshift.

Same with a vehicle pulling off. As soon as you see the turn signal, foot off the gas. Coast or brake gently until it leaves the road. Either way, your CLEAR ZONE should keep you safely behind until the other vehicle either joins or leaves traffic.

When someone tries to pass you in a two-lane situation, as soon as they move out to pass, foot off the gas until they're back in the lane in front of you. This is one of the most helpful and important ways to SHARE THE ROAD.

When you're following another vehicle at 55 on a two-lane highway, you have to be extra careful. You must allow yourself enough room to stop if they stop or pull off suddenly.

Don't rely on other drivers to use their turn signals. Some people don't signal properly. Or they will make a sudden turnoff because they don't know exactly where it is. So always be aware of the distance between you and the vehicle ahead. If that distance begins to shorten, whether or not you see signals or even brake lights, react accordingly. Your safe following distance should be based on the Three-Second Rule. Again, whatever the speed, it should take at least three seconds for you to reach the same spot as the vehicle in front of you. That's a _minimum_ distance. At this stage, don't follow more closely than that.

Remember how to calculate it: As soon as the front vehicle crosses a landmark, like a road sign or a tree or an overpass, begin counting slowly ("one-one thousand, two-one thousand..."). If you can count to three, you're far enough behind.

Many drivers these days fail to maintain a safe following distance. Many drivers also speed. Chances are, if you're traveling on a two-lane highway with a speed limit of 55, other vehicles are going to pull up close behind you.

When this happens, don't be nervous. Do as follows:

— Maintain your speed. Don't slow down or speed up. Be consistent and predictable.

— If there is no traffic ahead of you, and the roadway is generally clear of hazards, the vehicle behind you will be waiting for an opportunity to pass. Most high-speed two-lane roads have a double yellow line down their middles. Passing zones either have a single broken line, or a solid line left/broken line right combination. As soon as you reach a passing zone, and the left lane is free of oncoming traffic, ease up on the gas and let the tailing vehicle pass.

— If you have traffic ahead, or if there are lots of curves or hills or hazards on the road — or both — make sure you continue to maintain your clear zone. If the vehicle behind you is following too closely and continues to do so, do one of two things:

1. Look for the first opportunity to pull over, put your turn signal on and ease off the lane until you are passed.

2. If there is nowhere to pull over, and the tailgater persists, put your emergency flashers on until he or she backs off. If this doesn't work, ease off the gas and move as far right as possible until the vehicle passes.

Do NOT hit your brakes in an effort to frustrate a tailgater. It is a dangerous thing to do. It could cause a collision, or it could trigger an angry confrontation. And don't try to correct another driver. If people are behaving unsafely, _avoid_ them.

If you see one vehicle passing another in the distance and approaching you, take your foot off the gas. Ease up until the passing vehicle is back in the oncoming lane. Make sure your low-beams are on to maximize your visibility to oncoming traffic.

TWO-LANE PASSING

Which brings us to passing. In a word: don't. You're not ready for this maneuver just yet. Passing another vehicle on a high-speed two-lane road is very difficult. It requires a lot of skill.

TWO-LANE PASSING REQUIRES OVERTAKING ANOTHER VEHICLE AND RETURNING TO THE RIGHT LANE BEFORE ONCOMING TRAFFIC REACHES YOU. A <u>VERY</u> DIFFICULT MANEUVER.

The closing speed between two vehicles, each traveling 55, is about 160 feet per _second._ You're going to need about ten seconds to pass another vehicle, which means you need a minimum of 1600 feet. That's almost one-third of a mile!

LEARN THE LIMITS

Do _not_ attempt to pass unless you encounter a slow-moving vehicle, and only then if you are absolutely sure the way ahead is clear. Also make sure you can pass before the passing zone ends. If so, do _all_ of the following:

1. Make sure passing is permitted. The road will have either a broken center line or a combination with the broken line on the right.

2. Be sure to check your blind spot in case someone behind you has already moved out to pass.

3. Make sure the vehicle in front of you is not about to make a turn — especially a left turn.

4. Signal as soon as you make the decision.

5. Accelerate strongly until you are out in front of the next vehicle. On a two-lane road, you should be going at least 10 miles an hour faster than it is.

6. Don't move back until you can see both headlights in the rearview mirror.

7. Don't slow down until you are back in the right lane.

8. Don't swerve. Signal and move over quickly but smoothly.

9. Ease back to your cruising speed.

10. If for some reason (oncoming traffic has appeared, for example) you decide not to pass, signal and ease back behind the other vehicle. Never try to force your way in front of it.

11. Again, don't pass unless you are absolutely sure it's safe.

And don't pass another vehicle at all if it's moving close to the speed limit. Wait until you've been driving at least six months before you attempt this maneuver.

STEP SEVEN:

| PARENTS |

NIGHT DRIVING

Night driving is different from daytime driving, although the same skills apply to both.

The variations include:

— learning when to turn headlights on

— learning when to use high and low beams

— avoiding "overdriving" headlights

— dealing with headlights from oncoming and overtaking vehicles

— noticing reflections, contrast, and movement

For Step Seven, you should use the same locations that were visited in Steps Three through Six. Return to the places you used in daylight, and let your teen practice at dusk and at night.

You can skip the beginning parking lot and the back streets. Start with the neighborhood roads, move to the commercial strip, then on to the country roads, lightly-traveled highways, and high-speed two-lane blacktops.

| TEENS |

LIGHTS ON

Many drivers delay too long turning their headlights on. They figure that if they still can see the road well, there's no reason to turn the lights on. But headlights have

two purposes. Not only are they meant to help you see when it's dark, they are meant to help other drivers see you.

You should follow three rules regarding headlights:

1. Turn your low-beams on as soon as the sun goes down. (Sometimes this is called "the magic hour.")

2. Turn them on if the daytime weather is heavily over-cast (which includes rain and snow) or foggy.

3. Turn them on any time you are traveling a two-lane road with a 55-mile-an-hour speed limit.

LOW-BEAMS

Low-beams are aimed low and to the right. They are meant to accommodate both you and oncoming drivers while you are passing each other.

They also should be used if you see a pedestrian walking in your direction. Even if someone is on a sidewalk, if he or she is facing you, your high-beams can be blinding.

In heavy traffic, use low-beams only.

HIGH-BEAMS

High-beams are aimed higher and more toward the center of the road. They give you maximum visibility, but they can also be blinding to other drivers.

As soon as you see headlights approaching you, dim your lights. If the other driver fails to dim also, flash your high-beams _briefly_. If you are ignored, _don't_ put your high-beams back on. Keep your eyes lowered and to the right of the roadway until the other vehicle passes.

Flash your high-beams at trucks and trailers if they pass you as soon as there's room for them to pull back into the right lane. This is an especially valuable courtesy at night. Most truckers will flash their running lights back at you to say "thanks."

HEADLIGHT LIMITS

You need to be aware that it is possible to "overdrive" your headlights. That is, you can be going fast enough that your stopping distance is farther than your headlights can see. If an unexpected hazard appears, you may not be able to stop in time.

If you stay at 55 and under, this is usually not a problem on a straight road. On hills and curves, you should be using your CLEAR ZONE to govern your speed anyway, just as you would in daytime.

'ICE CREAM'

There is a good general strategy for driving at night. Three things almost always indicate a hazard or cause for attention:
— contrast
— reflection
— movement

They are the inconsistencies that were discussed in Step Four.

Inconsistencies: contrast, reflection and movement.

I = C.R.M.

Think "ice cream."

If you pick up inconsistencies early, you can deal with them. Everything's sweet, like ice cream. But if you miss something and a hazard appears in front of you suddenly, you'll be thinking something else: "I scream!"

Anything that reflects your headlights brightly should attract your attention:

— the reflective surface of a road sign, which you will want to read

— a piece of glass or metal on or beside the road, which you want to avoid

— reflective striping on a cyclist or pedestrian or pet collar

— the eyes of an animal, like a deer or raccoon

In all these cases, reflections are something to be noticed.

Likewise, contrast could indicate something lying in the road, or a pothole. And movement is always something that should attract your attention immediately.

As you drive at night, the passing road and landscape take on a particular pattern. As long as the pattern remains consistent, you can remain relaxed and proceed at a steady rate. Whenever something appears that is inconsistent — like contrast, reflection, or movement — you should instantly raise your attention level. Focus on that inconsistency until you identify it and decide how to react to it.

Most of the time, you will not have to react at all. It's just that you never want to ignore an inconsistency.

DON'T FORGET, LIGHTS OFF

Once you get into the habit of turning your lights on, you also need to remember to turn them off. This should not be a problem at night, because it's easy to tell when they're on.

But there are conditions during the day when you need to turn them on as well. By the time you reach your destination, the weather may have improved, or you may have forgotten they're on.

If you leave your headlights on for more than an hour or so, they could drain the battery to the point where you can no longer start the vehicle. Your vehicle may not have a lights-on warning tone or an automatic shutoff, so you could walk away and return later to a dead battery.

Here's a simple way to avoid this: any time you park and begin walking away, get into the habit of looking back at your vehicle. Just take a few steps and look back. You'll notice immediately if your lights are still on.

STEP EIGHT:

PARENTS

CITY STREETS

This is a variation of Steps Three and Four, involving heavy, slow-moving traffic in stop-and-go situations, except that in urban areas, you have the added complication of narrow lanes, many more pedestrians, and spillovers at intersections.

There isn't much new to learn here in terms of rules or special skills. But streets are more challenging than parking lots. While it's important to expose your teen to dense city traffic, you also need to wait until he or she has gained some overall experience. Hence, city driving follows country highway driving.

You will need to watch out for the following situations:

— tight lane squeezes

— crowding from trucks and buses

— doors suddenly opening on parked vehicles

— spillover traffic at intersections

— drivers trying to turn through clogged lanes

— uneven pavement and sudden changes in street conditions

— one-way streets

Continue co-piloting and spend at least a half-dozen sessions in city traffic. Concentrate on getting your teen to THINK AHEAD. It's the fourth of the five themes — making the right decisions ahead of time to avoid awkward maneuvers and situations.

Make sure your teen gains some experience dealing with one-way streets, both driving on them and turning onto them. Make sure he or she recognizes "One Way" and "Do Not Enter" signs. Don't take it for granted. All this is still new.

And while you're in the city, it's finally time to begin lessons in parallel parking. Your teen has been driving long enough now that this should not be a major challenge.

When I started teaching my daughters, they both seemed very worried about the prospect of parallel parking. So I postponed it until late in the instruction. Then I told them something that erased their anxiety: how difficult can anything be that you do at one mile an hour?

TEENS   STEADY, STRAIGHT AND CALM

City driving can rattle even the most experienced of us. The volume of activity, coupled with the tension and quick tempers that many people naturally display in this environment, can create unpleasant and frustrating experiences.

By now, you've been exposed to most of the basic situations you will encounter — though in greater numbers and frequency — in the city. You should know, for example, that when you're traveling in traffic on a narrow lane, you should focus ahead to help you hold a steady line. This will be particularly useful when you're traveling beside a bus or a large truck.

You also should know to CLEAR THE WAY ahead, so if you're passing a long line of parked cars, you're constantly noticing whether any of them is about to pull out. Someone also might open a door suddenly to get out.

Theme Four of Five:
THINK AHEAD

There's also something new to learn here. It's the fourth of the five themes: THINK AHEAD.

It sounds simple. It is. It's also very important in tight

traffic situations. It means always trying to keep in mind what you need to do well ahead of time, so you can avoid sudden moves, interference with others, or inconvenient mistakes.

Examples:

— You need to make a left turn ahead. But you are in the wrong lane. Solution: don't wait. Signal and move over as soon as there's an opening.

— Even though traffic ahead is jammed up, you continue to move forward into an intersection. You get stuck there when the light changes and now you are blocking cross traffic. Solution: make sure there is enough room for you to get through an intersection before you enter. If not, wait behind the stop line for a space to clear ahead.

— You are stopped at a stop light in front of an alley or parking lot entrance. An oncoming vehicle wants to turn left into that space but can't because you are blocking it. Solution: any time you see a traffic clog or a stop light ahead, make sure you don't block an _entrance_. An exit is another story. It's nice to leave an exit open, but not necessary. If there's room, allow a waiting vehicle to pull out in front of you as soon as traffic ahead begins moving.

In these examples, you needed to THINK AHEAD. Try to recognize such situations before they develop. As long as you do, you can be the best possible city driver: steady, straight and calm. You become invisible in the sea of vehicles, because you aren't making any sudden movements and you aren't holding up anybody else.

PARALLEL PARKING

Sooner or later, you're going to have to parallel park. A lot of teens seem to consider this the ultimate driving challenge. It really isn't much. Think about it. How hard could it be if you're moving so slowly?

Here are the basics:

1. When you see a space, slow down, put your turn signal on and pull beside the vehicle in front of the space.

2. Make sure the traffic behind you is stopped or pulling around before you begin backing up.

3. Divide the space into imaginary thirds. Using the back end of your vehicle as a reference, steer into the space at the two-thirds mark at about a 45-degree angle.

4. When your back end is mostly inside the space, begin to straighten out inside the space, but keep an eye on the vehicle beside you to avoid scraping it with your front fender.

5. Keep backing up until your back end is nearly touching the vehicle behind you, straightening out as much as possible.

6. Pull up so you end up in the center of the space. That's it!

Back up very slowly at first. It will help you position the vehicle properly. Remember to steer only when you're moving, unless the space is so tight there's no choice.

GUIDE YOUR VEHICLE'S REAR END INTO THE SPACE TO MATCH THE FRONT END OF THE VEHICLE BEHIND YOU. THEN STRAIGHTEN OUT.

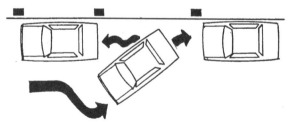

If you've parked well, the vehicle should be about six inches from the curb. Farther away and you risk sticking out into the street where you could be sideswiped. Closer in and it becomes difficult to pull back out. Also, you could scrape your tires and wheel covers on the curb.

Be patient through this. It may take several tries before your teen gets it right. You may want to begin on a quiet side street, so the maneuver can be practiced without worrying about traffic.

Do it on both sides of the street. Start on the right side, of course, but as soon as the teen begins to handle it well, find a one-way street with parallel parking and work on pulling into a space on the left side.

STEP NINE:
INTO HEAVY TRAFFIC

This is the most difficult step in the series because it introduces your teen to the most serious problem on our highways: heavy traffic at high speeds. It is where impatience and lack of skill and emotional outbursts produce continually hazardous conditions. Everyone is at risk here, no matter how competent.

Even if the previous steps have gone well, you may want to postpone Step Nine until your teen has obtained his or her license and has been driving for several more months.

Driving on urban interstate highways and other heavy traffic situations is quite different from any other experiences your teen has had so far. It requires a high attention level and very strong skills to keep safe.

Again, it's not thinking that's needed so much as heightened senses and proper attitude. The driver must be constantly alert and relaxed at the same time.

Too much thinking in this situation causes fatigue. And fatigue lowers reaction time and causes accidents. There is a vast difference between being inattentive and preoccupied and being a detached and relaxed driver.

I am inclined to take a position here similar to the one about keeping teens under 55 for the first year and not allowing them to pass on high-speed two-lane roads. Spend a lot of time training in heavy highway traffic. But even after the license, don't let him or

111

her go it alone for a while. There simply has not been enough time for all the necessary skills to develop.

HEAVY STUFF

There are three approaches to driving in heavy highway traffic. The first is to drive aggressively, with little regard for others on the road. Aggressive drivers move at excessive speed at every opportunity. They weave in and out of lanes, always striving to get out in front.

It is an extremely unsafe approach. It endangers everyone who is nearby, and it can even elicit copycat reactions in other drivers. The huge toll in life and limb that aggression and speed take on the roads each year is testimony to the folly of this approach. Add the effects of alcohol, and the results are truly tragic.

To get an idea of the scale of the carnage, think about the last time you watched a well-attended professional baseball game, either at the ballpark or on TV. Crowds at such events usually total around 40,000. That's about the size of one year's fatalities on our highways. A ballpark full of people!

The second approach is what I see being followed by most people on today's highways. It's a form of pack mentality. There's a euphemism that you hear frequently. It's called "keeping up with traffic." This means that no matter what the speed limit is, drivers go with the flow.

Pack driving also is unsafe, because of the tone of aggression in the packs. Everyone is trying to push through the group. As a result, the general speed increases and the distances between vehicles diminish. Sooner or later, someone makes a misjudgment and things can go wrong very quickly. At the very least, it becomes an annoyance for everyone else, because traffic is stopped or must move through a bottleneck until the crash is cleared.

Some of the worst traffic pile-ups in history have resulted from the packs, especially when visibility is low or the road surface is slippery, or both.

LIGHT STUFF

The third approach is the one I practice and recommend. It doesn't involve poking along either, which also can be a dangerous practice, because it elicits frustration and anger in other drivers.

I have a name for it: LIGHTFOOTING.

It is a way to drive in traffic without participating in the packs or becoming caught up in the pressures. The technique is very simple, and it can work for you whether you're a beginner or a veteran. It involves doing one of two things: drive the speed limit, or drive slightly slower than the pack, whichever speed is lower. It may seem strange to say you should hang back a little. You probably have heard the opposite from everyone else.

There is a common complaint about driving in traffic that I have heard for years. You may have heard it, too. It goes something like this:

"The drivers on so-and-so highway are crazy. They won't let you go the speed limit. You have to go 10 to 15 miles an hour over the limit just to keep up!"

Baloney. No one forces you to speed. I have never — repeat, NEVER — been in a situation where I felt forced to drive over the speed limit. That's not to say I haven't done it once in a while. I'm no saint. I've made my share of mistakes. But they _were_ mistakes. And I don't mean I refused to drive faster even though other drivers were trying to move me along. In a two-lane situation, whenever I pick up a tailgater, I move to the right at the first opportunity and let him or her pass.

Never, never, deliberately hold anyone back. It will make them extremely angry. Many tailgaters erupt into rage very quickly if they believe someone is blocking them. This is a serious act that could cause a crash or a violent confrontation on the road.

I'm talking about driving at a pace that is not only safe for conditions, but *considerate* of others on the road.

IT'S RELATIVE

The key to safe driving in traffic is not the particular speed of your vehicle, but the relative speed. Also important is the rate of change in speed and direction.

In other words, you must maintain a safe speed relative to your vehicle and the others on the road:

— How fast are you accelerating and decelerating?

— How suddenly are you changing lanes or directions?

All of this sums up in one word: predictability.

Everybody on the road needs to feel reasonably certain about what everybody else is doing. As long as this situation prevails, so does safety. But when packs of vehicles increase their speed, with each vehicle jockeying to get ahead, and with not much distance among them, predictability disappears very quickly.

The way to remain safe is to travel at a very steady speed, with gradual shifts in lane, acceleration, and deceleration. As long as you practice this, stay approximately at the speed limit, *and* avoid blocking the passing lanes, you will have no trouble in the heaviest of traffic.

The highways are full of speeders, true. But they tend to use the passing lanes. Staying to the right except when passing allows you to LIGHTFOOT without interfering with the LEADFEET.

114

HEAVY TRAFFIC SKILLS

In this step, your teen needs to practice all the skills taught in the other steps. The main difference is that the conditions will be much more challenging.

The skills include:

— merging into and exiting out of the traffic flow
— maintaining a good line
— passing
— maintaining proper following distance
— accelerating and braking within traffic

There are also three new skills to develop:

— predicting and reacting to the pack behavior of drivers
— detecting traffic clogs ahead
— passing through narrow lanes in construction zones

Extreme care is needed for every one of these situations. If you have any doubts, postpone this step. Don't subject a young driver to heavy, high-speed traffic until he or she is ready. And don't allow solo driving in these conditions for at least one year *after* the license has been obtained.

When your teen is ready, find a major traffic artery and map out a course along it. Where I live, in Northern Virginia, just outside Washington, D.C., we have the notorious "Beltway." It is an eight-lane highway running some 60 miles around the city. It takes about an hour and a quarter to complete one loop. That's about right for these lessons.

If you don't have a similar roadway, just take a stretch of 30 miles or so along an expressway and travel it in both directions. You and your teen will have to make dozens of trips along the route before basic competence begins to appear.

| TEENS | TIGHT MERGES

Merging into traffic is complicated. You have to scan the traffic, pick your entrance spot, move your vehicle into

position, and avoid running out of ramp.

But there _is_ a way to simplify things. First, make sure there is a merge ramp, also called an acceleration lane. Some older highways have very short ramps. Some even have none at all. Don't _assume_ you have room. Be certain.

Next, determine how much room you have on the ramp. If there is plenty, merging becomes a question of getting up to the speed of the traffic, turning your signal on as soon as you're visible to oncoming vehicles, choosing your merge slot, and moving into it. Chances are, if you're moving at the right speed, someone in the lane will let you in. Just be sure the slot is there before you take it.

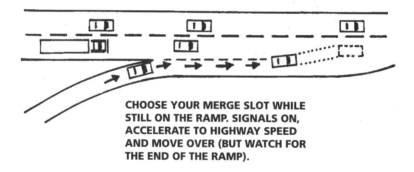

CHOOSE YOUR MERGE SLOT WHILE STILL ON THE RAMP. SIGNALS ON, ACCELERATE TO HIGHWAY SPEED AND MOVE OVER (BUT WATCH FOR THE END OF THE RAMP).

On the other hand, if the merge ramp is short, you've got to THINK AHEAD. You must find your merge slot before you run out of ramp. What if you can't find one? Cut back on your speed _early_ on the ramp until you see a slot. Then accelerate and move into it. Don't stop. Slow to a crawl if you must, but don't stop.

What if you have no choice but to stop? Some highways now have "metered" access. A stop light on the ramp alternates rapidly between red and green, allowing one or two vehicles at a time to enter. When the lights are activated, however, traffic is usually so heavy it has slowed way down. And the lights are usually positioned well up the ramp, to give drivers the opportunity to accelerate.

Worst case: no ramp, no room. Then, you have no alternative. Pull up to the stopping place. If traffic is slow, ease in. If it's high speed, you're going to have to wait until you have enough room to move over _and_ get up to speed. If traffic is moving at 55, that's 80 feet a second. You will need at least five seconds to merge under these conditions. That's 400 feet of space.

The good news is that worst case merges are rare. Most of the time, you should be able to find a slot and move into it without causing a disruption of traffic flow or scaring yourself to death. Just remember the rules.

MIXING LOOPS

Many highways now have "mixing loops" at interchanges. They are exit and entrance lanes joined by a loop at the center from an overpass or underpass. Mixing loops can be tricky because they contain traffic that is entering and exiting the highway at the same time. If you're entering, you must merge with exiting traffic that is moving faster and trying to cross over into your lane.

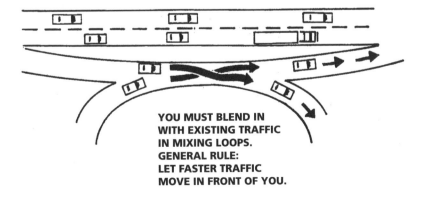

YOU MUST BLEND IN WITH EXISTING TRAFFIC IN MIXING LOOPS. GENERAL RULE: LET FASTER TRAFFIC MOVE IN FRONT OF YOU.

There are no easy rules here. And mixing loops are frequent sites of crashes. So be careful. Focus your attention on the loop lane until you're parallel to the acceleration/deceleration lane. Then do one of two things:

1. If exiting traffic is overtaking you, let it cut in front of you.

2. If you're clear, signal and move over. Exiting traffic should let you cross in front. Watch out, however, for drivers who use mixing loops to cut ahead of traffic on the highway. They create a very dangerous situation.

When you exit on a mixing loop, use common sense and courtesy:

— If you overtake a vehicle in the loop, signal and move over in front.

— If the vehicle is beside you or in front of you, ease up and slip in behind it.

BLENDING IN

In Step Six, we covered changing lanes, passing, being passed, and maintaining enough stopping distance. It's basically the same here, with one important difference: most of the time, you'll be surrounded by other vehicles, all trying to do many of the same things.

Here is where you have to learn basic traffic survival. You have to blend in.

SHARE THE ROAD.

Blending has two components:

— reacting to what's happening

— whenever possible, letting others by

If everyone were courteous, the roads would be much, much safer. But courtesy doesn't seem to be on the minds of many motorists. That doesn't mean it shouldn't be practiced, however. Just be aware of what the other drivers around you are trying to do.

Somebody ahead trying to merge? Let them in. If there's room, move over a lane so they can have an easy time finding their merge slot.

Somebody trying to pass? Let them by. Stay in the right lane when you're not passing, or move to the right as soon as you can.

Somebody wants to change lanes? Let them change lanes, even if they're behaving aggressively or unsafely. Don't increase tension or add to the problem by getting in their way.

It's that simple. But you will need time to develop a sense of what's going on with the other drivers.

DON'T PASS ON THE RIGHT

Passing in the right lane has become very common on highways, especially in heavy traffic. But it's illegal and dangerous. Don't fall into the habit. Use the left lane for passing and the right lane for cruising.

WATCH OUT FOR WEAVERS

It's also very common in traffic to encounter lane weavers, drivers that change lanes frequently and rapidly. In a typical situation, you will be overtaken by a vehicle that is being followed by a lane weaver. As soon as there is enough space between you and the front vehicle, the weaver will dart to the right and in front of you.

This is another illegal and dangerous activity. The best thing for you to do, however, is stay out of it. If you see a weaver approaching in your mirror, ease off the gas to allow the quickest possible opportunity for that vehicle to get by you.

BETTER BEHIND THAN AHEAD

Something important to remember: whenever you're dealing with aggressive or unsafe drivers, the best place to be is behind them. As long as you are following, you are in a position to react to them and protect yourself. You can't do much if they're behind you.

HOLDING THE LINE

Moving in heavy traffic, you may find it difficult to hold the vehicle in a steady line. That's what will happen if you limit your attention to the vehicle immediately in front of you.

You need to keep a wider focus. As much as possible, look through the vehicle ahead, and use the visual clues that the roadway, the guardrails and the landscape provide. Remember, your hands will follow your eyes.

If you keep your attention well ahead, it will also alert you to a common traffic situation that can become dangerous very quickly: the traffic clog. There are many causes. Like a crash ahead, or a problem with the roadway. Sometimes, traffic becomes so heavy that the roadway simply runs out of room. Traffic clogs to a stop.

You need to be alert to clusters of brakelights appearing ahead. They mean traffic is slowing down or stopping for some reason. You want to spot clogs as soon as possible because you don't want to be caught in a chain reaction pile-up. That's when somebody stops suddenly and is hit from behind by someone who couldn't react in time, and who in turn is hit from behind, and so on.

Anytime you see a cluster beginning — it almost always appears as a relay of brakelights heading back toward you — take your foot off the gas and prepare to slow down or stop. Touch your brake pedal gently to alert drivers behind you.

NARROW LANES

One other difficult and potentially dangerous situation you will eventually encounter on highways — especially heavily-traveled ones — is shifted and narrow lanes due to construction. At most road construction sites, speed limits are reduced to help traffic travel safely through the disrupted area. Many drivers speed through them, however, just like they speed everywhere else. This can be very unnerving.

The key to navigating narrow lanes, as in so many other highway and traffic situations, is to keep your attention well ahead. But you'll have to concentrate even harder to maintain a good line. Try to keep everything else out of your mind while you're driving through a construction zone. Concentrate on staying in the center of the lane.

One last caution: always be extremely careful around highway construction workers. They have one of the most dangerous jobs in America (or anywhere else). Foot off the gas anytime you see them near the roadside. Give them as much room as you can.

STEP TEN:

PARENTS   COPING WITH BAD WEATHER

You and your teen may have to wait quite a while to complete all the lessons in Step Ten for obvious reasons. On the other hand, it isn't necessary for him or her to master every facet of bad-weather driving before obtaining a license. Just don't let the student drive in heavy rain, fog, or especially ice and snow unless he or she has spent some time in it under your supervision.

Depending upon your location and climate, it may take an entire year to practice in all types of bad weather. Or you never may have to worry about frozen roads. Either way, the first year or so should be considered an instruction period. So whether the license has been obtained or not, whenever the forecast calls for fog, rain, snow or ice, try to plan a practice session. It may sound strange, but you can use bad weather to your advantage.

REPEAT (MOSTLY) EVERYTHING IN HEAVY WEATHER

When clouds gather, you should repeat Steps Three through Nine, in that order. Allow your teen to become familiar with the aspects of bad weather starting out in less intense conditions. Even such basics as using windshield wipers and washers and the defoggers ought to be practiced away from traffic at first.

You also should return to the empty parking lot because it can be beneficial during snow and ice. You can practice skidding there in the safety of open space.

Everything your teen has learned under fair skies ought to be repeated in bad weather. Go back through the neighborhoods, the commercial strips and parking garages, country roads, city streets, and the highways, both uncrowded and crowded. Go back through as much of it as you can, day and night, using the guidelines for rain, snow, ice and fog.

TEENS   FIRST RULE: LIGHTS ON

As mentioned in Step Eight, any time the skies darken, you should turn your lights on immediately. Remember, it's just as important to be seen as to see. Your headlights make your vehicle much more visible, especially at a distance.

DEALING WITH FOG

Fog usually doesn't change road conditions. It only limits visibility. That's a potentially hazardous condition, but it's a simple one to deal with:

Make your vehicle as visible as possible to everyone else, and slow down until your speed matches your CLEAR ZONE.

In light and moderate fog, turn your lights on — low beams only. Fog reflects high-beams with a lot of glare and actually will reduce your vision. If your vehicle is equipped with fog lights, use them as well.

If you are traveling on a high-speed highway and fog forces you to slow down more than 10 miles an hour under the speed limit, turn your flashers on as well. They will alert traffic behind you that you are not traveling at normal speed.

Follow everything you have learned about creating a CLEAR ZONE. Slow down until your zone matches your speed. Do this even if it means slowing down to a crawl. Most fog-related accidents happen because drivers fail to match their speed to their ability to see.

Be especially aware of what's going on behind you. Many drivers are just as careless in fog as they are in clear weather. They drive too fast for conditions. If you see headlights approaching from behind, make sure they are slowing down as they get closer to you. If not, turn your flashers on. If that doesn't work, pull over. Let 'em by.

Remember, you're better off behind a careless driver.

RAINY DAYS

You might think (my second-favorite song by The Cars, by the way) that rain doesn't change the rules of driving much. After all, it's only water. But there are several ways rain can make streets and roads more hazardous:

1. It reduces your vision, mostly because of the rain itself, and partly because darkened skies make it more difficult to see distant objects.

123

2. It reduces friction on the roadway. Stopping distance becomes greater and you could skid on curves.

3. In heavy amounts, it creates the possibility of flash flooding, which can trap you in low-lying areas.

You always should treat rain with respect. It will present you with new challenges and experiences. Even light rain can increase your stopping distance.

GET USED TO THE WIPERS

Simple and silly as it may seem, looking through your windshield with your wipers on may take some getting used to. Some people find wipers a major distraction. You have to train yourself to ignore them by concentrating your attention on the road ahead.

You also need to learn how often to use your wipers. Almost all vehicles now have variable interval wiper controls. Too fast and they may start screeching annoyingly across the glass. Too slow and they won't clear off the rain fast enough to keep your vision clear. There's no ideal frequency for wipers. It depends on conditions.

Whenever it begins to rain, unless it's a heavy downpour, use your windshield washer the first time you turn your wipers on. Stuff constantly is accumulating on your windshield, so if you turn your wipers on to wipe off a few raindrops, chances are you will create smears across the glass. Clean the glass and the wiper blades with the washers at the beginning.

USE YOUR VEHICLE'S CLIMATE CONTROLS

Increased humidity that is associated with rain, snow and fog can affect your vision from inside the vehicle as well. Differences in temperature between the air inside and outside cause tiny water droplets to condense on the windshield inside. As soon as you see this happening, turn on your vehicle's defogger. If the weather is warm or only moderately cold, you may need to use the air conditioner as well, because it dehumidifies the interior air. In colder weather, use the defogger with the heater.

Use your rear window defogger if necessary, but remember to turn it off as soon as the window is clear. If the weather is very cold, you may need to defrost the windshield and rear window before starting out.

Always make sure your windows are clear before you attempt to drive anywhere. That also means taking the time to clean snow and ice off all your windows — and outside mirrors — before you move the vehicle.

Something else to remember: if you need to adjust temperature or airflow controls on the instrument panel, be very careful. If you shift your attention from the road to the interior of the vehicle, you will be traveling blind for as long as it takes. Even a five-second diversion at 35 miles an hour means you will travel 250 feet without looking. Any time you fail to CLEAR THE WAY, you are asking for trouble. So try to make adjustments at stop lights or stop signs, or make sure the road is clear far ahead before looking down for no more than a second or two.

RAINY NIGHTS

Night driving in the rain can be especially challenging because rain on the windshield scatters the light of oncoming headlights, irritating your eyes and making it difficult to see ahead. Rain also changes the reflective patterns of the roadway, so that the outline of the lanes may become poorly defined.

You have to be especially careful to maintain an effective CLEAR ZONE in front of you, and to watch for "Ice Cream" — inconsistencies of contrast, reflection and movement. Adjust your speed to compensate for reduced vision _and_ the increased stopping distance required by the wet pavement.

TRUCK WAVES

Whenever you encounter large trucks on highways on very rainy days, you need to watch out for their bow waves. These are heavy zones of water that extend at an angle from both sides of the front of the trucks. They can blind you temporarily, even if your wipers are working at maximum speed.

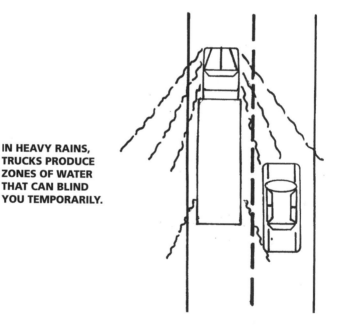

IN HEAVY RAINS, TRUCKS PRODUCE ZONES OF WATER THAT CAN BLIND YOU TEMPORARILY.

If a truck is about to pass you, or you are about to pass a truck, make sure you CLEAR THE WAY far ahead and know exactly which way the road is going, because your vision will be obscured for a few seconds.

If you are being passed, ease off the gas for a moment until the bow wave clears you. If you are passing, accelerate through it, but _gently_. Too much power on a very wet road could send you into a skid.

WATER ON THE ROADWAY

When the road gets wet, the water acts as a lubricant. It reduces the ability of your tires to cling to the pavement. Stopping distance is increased, and the road provides less friction to overcome your vehicle's inertia going around curves. Too fast, and you could slide, either off the road or into oncoming traffic. This is true especially during the first few minutes of a rainstorm. The water hitting the roadway mixes with oil and grime that have accumulated on the surface. Until the surface slick is washed away, the pavement can be very slippery.

When rain becomes heavy, and you are traveling at highway speeds, you could encounter a dangerous phenomenon called hydroplaning. Your vehicle's tires are designed with grooves in the tread. The grooves serve several purposes, one of which is to act as channels for water on the roadway. When they work properly, the tire tread grips the road and water is squeezed into the grooves.

In heavy rain, however, there's so much water on the pavement that the grooves can't hold it all. When this happens, the tires lose contact. The vehicle actually begins to float on the water, and you lose steering and stopping control.

Another rain-related hazard: wet leaves on the roadway. They can be very slippery and can send you into a skid if you encounter them on a curve or if you try to stop on them.

Maybe the most hazardous condition of all is water flowing across a roadway — flash-flooding. You may not know this, but more people are killed in the U.S. by floods than by any other type of weather-related cause. Many of them drown in vehicles because they try to cross flooded roadways and are trapped or swept away by rising waters.

Keep all this in mind when you start out on a rainy day. Rain changes the rules. It narrows the _limits_ of what you can do. You need to proceed carefully until you LEARN THE LIMITS.

Theme Five of Five:
FEEL THE ROAD

How should you handle these conditions? The best way is to avoid them. That's easy in the case of flooding:

Don't try to cross a flooded roadway. Even if you can see the pavement under a couple of inches of water, the flow could have undermined the roadbed. You could get stuck in a sinkhole. Don't risk it. Turn back and find an alternate route until the water level drops.

For the other conditions, it's extremely important to know immediately that the tires are losing traction with the road. If it happens, and you don't know it, you easily could lose control. That means instead of driving down the road, you are suddenly _riding_ inside a ton and a half or so of vehicle with a mind of its own. You could end up off the road, possibly upside down. Or you could collide with something: a tree, a lamp post, a barrier, or another vehicle.

You never want to be in this situation. The best way to prevent it is to stay home whenever it rains or snows. Okay, that's not practical. The second best way is to slow down in wet weather or icy conditions. That's good, but it may not always be enough. You must be able to detect loss of traction instantly. To do this, you have to FEEL THE ROAD.

This is the last of the five themes, and it is the most important thing to do whenever the pavement is wet or icy.

While you are driving, your brain is receiving various sensory inputs. Part of those inputs come from your hands on the steering wheel, your feet on the pedals, and your whole body sitting in the seat. In a way, you are connected to your vehicle, and it is connected to the road. From it, you sense direction, speed, acceleration and deceleration.

You must also learn to sense what the tires are doing. Several things can happen:

— You are driving in a straight line and suddenly your drive wheels start spinning faster than they should — your vehicle begins to "fish-tail."

— You are in a turn but you begin to slide toward the outside of the curve — your wheels are turned but you are moving straight ahead.

— You press the brake pedal but the vehicle doesn't slow down, and it begins to swerve sideways.

— You try to start but the wheels spin and the vehicle doesn't move.

In all but the last case, the results can be very dangerous if traction isn't restored immediately. The longer you go without reacting, the more likely you are to end up losing control.

So you must learn to sense when the tires are beginning to slip. How? The best way is to practice. But you can't just go out into traffic and practice. You need to start where your mistakes won't harm you or anyone else.

Go back to the parking lot.

Chances are, you won't be able to do much slipping and sliding in the parking lot when it's only raining. Your teen won't be able to drive fast enough to make much happen. The real test will come in snow and ice.

Still, it's very important if at all possible to practice skidding. Unless your teen can experience skidding under supervision, and learn to anticipate it and control it, he or she will remain at a disadvantage in many conditions.

Skidding should be practiced so that reacting to it becomes reflexive. If this has not happened before the license has been obtained, you need to place some limits on your teen's driving. No high-speed highways in rainy weather, for example, and no driving on snowy or icy roads at all.

BASIC SKID DRILLS

There are three types of skids:
—stopping skids
—turning skids
—power skids

The first two can be practiced in the parking lot. The third is better experienced on the open road. But if your teen becomes accustomed to the first two, and reads this section carefully, he or she should be able to react properly to the third if it occurs.

Wait for a heavy rain — or snow or ice if they're available — and return to the parking lot.

Begin as you did in Step One, with very basic movements. Before your teen can learn to control a skid, he or she must learn what a skid feels like. So start at one end of the lot, accelerate quickly, and stop hard at the other end. No steering, no control, just hit the brakes and see what happens. This drill may not be very useful if your vehicle is equipped with an antilock braking system (ABS). You may want to skip it and move on.

Try these free-style hard stops several times. Watch the student's reaction. Is he or she nervous? If so, continue the practice until things calm down a little.

Next, do some hard stops and have the student try to keep the vehicle headed in a straight line. What he or she quickly will discover is that steering while braking won't work (unless the vehicle has ABS). The brakes must be pumped gently while steering—but don't allow pumping with ABS.

Antilock brakes require steady pressure. They do the pumping for you. It's a technical advance meant to provide some control during a skid. Even so, there is no substitute for practice and experience. The empty parking lot forgives errors.

This may take more than one lesson to learn. Controlling a stopping skid requires quick hands and feet, and this takes a little time to develop. So spend time. Have the student work on it until he or she can do it consistently: slam on the brakes, go into a skid, and recover in a straight line.

TEENS   "F.Re.S.H."

Skidding might seem like something you should be afraid of. But if you follow the rules, you can avoid losing complete control of the vehicle.

Why do vehicles skid? When the road surface is slippery, the tires lose their ability to grip. When that happens, you can no longer control your direction or speed. Your vehicle might as well be on four ball bearings as four tires.

How do you overcome this? You have to react in the right combination:

Feel the skid beginning?

Remove your foot from the gas or the brake.

Steer to correct your Heading.

Just remember:

Feel, Remove, Steer, Heading

Head is the critical element here, in more ways than one. First, you want to keep yours. Stay cool. Don't panic if you feel a skid. You should know well by now that the first thing to do in just about any situation like this is take your foot off the gas.

You also need to keep your head pointed in the direction you want to go. As we discussed earlier, your hands will steer where you look.

It's a little more complicated when you're trying to slow down, because you need to take your foot off the brake, steer to correct, then resume braking, tapping the pedal rapidly until you stop.

In the case of antilock brakes, if you feel a skid, steer while braking. Don't pump the brakes. Hold the pedal down.

PARENTS   TURNING SKIDS

There are two ways to practice turning skids. First is to start out quickly with the wheels turned sharply. If the parking lot is wet enough, you should be able to skid on it. Second is to try a sharp turn at speed.

In both situations, you want your teen to correct for the skid. That's easy when they're starting out. All they have to do is ease off the gas and steer to straighten out.

The second skid is more difficult. At a high enough speed and a sharp enough turn, it is almost impossible to correct. But that's okay, because you want them to experience the situation. You want to condition them to it so they can avoid it on the roads.

Make sure there is plenty of room and no one else around when you try this.

Select a place in the lot with no obstructions or outside curbs, somewhere your teen can make a sharp turn without hit-

WHEN A SKID BEGINS, EASE OFF THE GAS AND STEER TOWARD YOUR ORIGINAL HEADING.

ting anything in case of a miss. The ideal situation is a racetrack-like course with two turns and two straightaways.

Start out at least 50 feet from the first turn and have the student accelerate toward it. The idea is to try to hold the course through it without slowing down.

Even if the surface is wet, the first try is likely to be messy. But you *want* the student to lose control.

Now start over and try again. You want your teen to accomplish three things here:

— becoming conditioned to the feel of a skid

— recovering from it

— sensing the proper speed to turn on a slippery surface so a skid can be avoided in the first place

This is serious business, but it also can be fun. In fact, it can be the most fun you'll have during this process. Because it's fun, spend a lot of time with it, especially if you can do it in snow or on ice. The more time your teen spends skidding in the parking lot, the more able he or she will be to anticipate a skid on the road and recover from it. The key is repeated exposure under controlled conditions.

POWER AND SPEED ARE ENEMIES

Rain, snow, and especially ice can reduce or even eliminate the traction between the road surface and your tires. That's why, on icy roads, you often see vehicles spinning their wheels loudly but going nowhere. The road has become too slippery for the tires to grip. Therefore the driver has difficulty controlling both momentum and direction.

Speed and power make things worse. The faster you go, the more inertia the vehicle builds up. Since you need friction with the road to overcome inertia, and since ice reduces friction, you will have less and less ability to overcome it. So if you try to turn at too high a speed, inertia will overcome the traction of your tires and you will slide sideways.

In the case of acceleration, if you use too much power, your drive wheels will begin slipping and will throw you into a condition called a power skid. The tires on your drive wheels spin freely, causing loss of control. This is a particularly dangerous situation, because it often happens at highway speeds.

The same with stopping. If you hit the brakes hard, the wheels can lock and the tires just slide across the surface.

Have you ever seen one of those bamboo finger torture devices sold at novelty shops? You put your index fingers in each side and try to pull them back out. But the harder you pull, the tighter it grips you. You can only escape if you pull out very slowly and gently.

It's the same with driving on slippery roads. When you step on the gas, you apply more power to the drive wheels. The engine spins the wheels faster. On dry pavement, this makes the vehicle go faster because of friction with the road. But on wet pavement, and especially on ice, the wheels just spin. When they do, there's no control.

So the number one tool you have for driving on slippery roads is low speed and gradual acceleration and deceleration. Driving gently provides control. Driving aggressively loses control. It's that simple.

WATCH OUT FOR BRIDGES

You may have noticed a strange road sign from time to time. It reads: "Bridge freezes before roadway," or some variation. It means that the road surface on the bridge could be icy, even though the surface over ground is not.

Sometimes, when the temperature drops rapidly, moisture on the roadway will not freeze because the roadbed is still relatively warm. It insulates the surface for a time and keeps it thawed. Since there is no warm thermal mass under a bridge, it will freeze more quickly. Hence, the road sign.

TEST THE ROAD

One of the most hazardous conditions on winter roads is rapid freezing of the pavement. You could be driving along with complete traction and then suddenly find yourself spinning out of control.

The way to avoid this is to test the road surface periodically. Every once in a while, hit your brakes briefly and see what happens. Just for a second, push hard on the pedal and see how much you slide. If it's a lot, you'll know to take it more slowly and carefully, and you'll be less likely to be surprised by a sudden icy patch.

Just make sure no other vehicles are around you when you try this, and do it only on a completely open and straight stretch of roadway.

ONE MORE WORD ABOUT POWER SKIDS

Sometimes, foot off the gas isn't enough. The minimum power still being delivered to the drive wheels may continue the skid. In certain situations, you will need to shift into neutral (or push in the clutch) to disconnect the power. On very slippery streets, you might have to do this often.

Your best strategy is still low speed. But if you misjudge, remember to disconnect power to the wheels.

| PARENTS | BACK ON THE ROADS |

Once your teen has gotten the hang of skidding in the parking lot, head back to the streets, roads and highways. The object there is not to skid, but to drive safely in bad weather. You want to work extensively on driving at the proper speed for conditions. That is the _best_ safe strategy. Then, if a skid does develop, your teen should be able to recover from it by following the procedures we've covered.

TEENS HEAVY SNOW

When snow accumulates on the roadway, you need to watch out for something else: getting stuck. It usually happens in three ways:

1. You are stuck where you have parked or are stopped.
2. You stop on a hill and can't start up again.

3. You slide off the road onto a soft shoulder or into a snowbank.

All three can be annoying and difficult. In the case of starting out, your best bet is to dig out the wheels and create a path to dry pavement. You should always carry a shovel with you during snowy weather, as well as something you can sprinkle under the wheels to aid traction. Cat litter is a popular substance for this use.

The next thing to do is try a technique called "rocking." You gently move the gearshift from drive to reverse in a regular rhythm until the vehicle becomes unstuck in one direction or the other. It's important to be gentle when you do this, because you don't want to damage the transmission. And remember the finger torture device. Don't stomp on the gas and make the wheels spin. Ease on and off the gas to keep the spinning to a minimum.

If you get stuck on a hillside, you may not be able to get started again. If possible, it's best to back down the hill, get a running start and try it again. Keep moving, but don't use so much power that you start a power skid. As soon as you feel the wheels start to spin, ease up.

If you slide off the road, and you can't dig yourself out, there may not be anything you can do except wait for a towtruck.

By the way, in cases where you're stuck, put down your window. Listen so you can tell more readily when your wheels start spinning.

THE BIGGEST DANGER

Even if you learn everything in this section perfectly, you still could be in danger in bad weather — from other drivers. Many people who are on slippery roads have very little skill in such conditions. And many of them fail to exercise even the most basic caution.

Along with everything else you have learned, remember especially to watch out for other drivers. It's more difficult to avoid them on slippery roads. Your best defense is to stay away from anybody who is driving too fast or recklessly, or appears to be unable to cope with conditions. On slippery roads, incompetent drivers can be just as dangerous as aggressive ones.

ON TO THE LICENSE (and then what?)

If your teen has completed the Ten Steps to Basic Skills — except for the heavy traffic and bad weather components, for example — it may be time to go for the license. In some states, that still means taking either a driver education class at school or paying for commercial instruction. But as I said at the beginning, either of these should be regarded as a legal requirement (and an annoying one at that) and not the best way to teach your youngster how to drive.

Before your teen takes the license exam, make sure he or she has studied the state's driver's manual, and is familiar with all the laws and technicalities that apply. It would be a shame to have spent all this time training, only to fail the written part of the test.

Assuming the state's material has been studied, escort your teen to the DMV, and celebrate when the test is passed. But before the vehicle gets taken out for the first time, discuss the limits that will apply over the next year or two while he or she explores the experiences of driving solo.

SENSIBLE LIMITS FOR YOUNG DRIVERS

As I also said at the beginning, developing good driving skills takes time. Teens will need to gain still more experience on the road before being permitted to go anywhere they please, whenever they please. This isn't just personal opinion. More and more states are enacting or considering graduated driving programs for teens, with strong support from insurance companies and parent organizations. These programs are meant to place reasonable limits on driving privileges for minors.

Even if such limits don't exist in your state or locality, you nevertheless should consider imposing them, especially during the first few months of the license. For instance:

— no driving over 55

— no passing on high-speed two-lane blacktop

— no high-speed heavy traffic

— no driving after midnight (and perhaps earlier on school nights)

— no passengers

It goes without saying, no drugs or alcohol. And seat belts are a requirement at all times.

There are very good reasons for all these restrictions. The first three have to do with experience. Highway speeds and heavy traffic require constant skill and judgment to assure relative safety. Even if you've spent many hours with your youngster in those conditions, more time is needed for him or her to mature. I recommend waiting until the youngster is at least seventeen before relaxing some of those restrictions.

The curfew rule is based on crash statistics. Teens are killed and injured late at night more than any other time. Part of it has to do with fatigue. Young people sometimes don't know their own limits. Part of it involves excessive speed and reduced visibility. Kids like to take risks, and sometimes those risks create situations they can't handle. And part of it, unfortunately, involves parties and alcohol. Keeping teens off the roads after midnight is an important way to help keep them safe.

There also is a horrible crash rate among teens who ride together. Those situations tend to involve a lot of noise and distractions for the driver. Whenever kids get into a car together, they naturally become rowdy. This also can encourage young drivers to take foolish risks. Peer presure prevails. Some of the worst highway tragedies have involved carloads of teens.

Many parents don't allow passengers during the first year of a license, and they don't allow their teens to ride with other teens. Both are good ideas. Take them very seriously.

POST-LICENSE CHECKUPS

Once the license is obtained, give your teen some time to develop on his or her own. All the material learned in the lessons must continue to be practiced. Even with the limits I've suggested, there should be plenty of opportunity to drive solo.

This doesn't mean, however, that your role as instructor is over. Every so often, ride along with your teen to see how well his or her skills are developing. For example, a month or so after the license, sit in for another driving session. This time, however, just be an observer, not a co-pilot.

Have your teen take you through the countryside, onto a highway, through a commercial strip and along some city streets. See how well he or she is managing. Is the driving steady and confident? Are the merges smooth? Is signaling used properly? And so on.

After the tour is over, discuss anything you noticed that needs attention. But also be complimentary about the things he or she performed well.

You'll still need to cover what you delayed or missed during the permit phase — especially heavy traffic and bad weather situations. Don't neglect them.

During the first year or so, there's an easy way to keep track of your teen's progress: any time you need to go somewhere together, have him or her drive. That way, you don't need to set up a special time — it doesn't have to seem like a lesson. It can become routine. And teens are usually happy to drive.

You also should let your teen drive on long trips. It's beneficial for both of you. It breaks up the monotony of the journey, and it's valuable experience for the novice driver. Try alternating every two hours, with a five- or ten-minute break in between. Two hours is about as long as anybody can drive non-stop without the effects of fatigue setting in. Stopping for short breaks at two-hour intervals is a very good habit to instill.

YOU STILL CAN SAY "NO"

Probably the most difficult aspect of parental responsibility involves disciplining a child when rules are broken. Just because the child is now a teenager with a driver's license doesn't change the basic situation. It still comes down to rules and consequences. What has changed is that the stakes have grown much, much higher.

Take the issue of teens driving teens. It has become common for high-schoolers to want to travel in groups, especially to social events or outings. As I mentioned in the Foreword, this can be a recipe for disaster. The odds of tragedy increase dramatically when teens pile into vehicles.

That's why more and more parents are prohibiting their kids from driving or riding with friends for at least one year after the license. If you choose to impose such a rule, and if your teen breaks it, there must be consequences. Here are two: (1) extend the no-passengers rule and/or (2) take back the car keys. The first one gets his or her attention. The second is called "hitting them where they live." A teen suddenly without wheels can be angry and sullen, but it's a good bet he or she will have gotten the message.

The same goes for breaking curfews. Just as the number of passengers increases the danger of a crash, time of day also is an important factor. After 10 p.m., the rate of teen-related crashes climbs dramatically. Imposing a curfew isn't an arbitrary decision. It's backed up by real numbers of real tragedies. Honoring a curfew is a sign of self-restraint and maturity. Breaking one tempts fate. Again: rules and consequences.

I know it's tough. I went through this with my own children. But as I said back in the Introduction, you remain legally responsible for the actions of your teen until he or she turns eighteen. Therefore, you must continue to convey to your teen that driving is a privilege that has to be taken seriously and performed responsibly. Lives are at stake. There is no other way of looking at it.

You _still_ can say "no."

CHOOSING A CAR FOR YOUR TEEN

Notice that I use the term "car" instead of "vehicle." I have a reason, and I'll get to it shortly.

There are several schools of thought about choosing a vehicle for a beginning driver. Many parents favor compact models for teens. They are popular because they are easy to handle and economical. And carmakers tend to promote them to young audiences as sporty.

But if you are considering such a vehicle — one with a wheel base of 100 inches or less — you should know that they are involved in twice as many fatal crashes as larger vehicles. Airbags, crumple zones, and other safety equipment notwithstanding, their lack of weight is a big drawback in a crash — and as we know, young teen drivers have crashes much more frequently than anyone else.

This category also includes the smaller versions of sport-utility vehicles, which seem to be very popular with teens. Manufacturers tout them as fun because they can travel across the countryside, along sandy beaches, up steep hills, and across shallow streams. But small sport-utility vehicles have high centers of gravity, and most are equipped with four-wheel drive. Both require additional driving skills that many teens lack. That's one reason why they are involved in nearly three times as many crash deaths as larger conventional cars. Pound for pound, they are the most dangerous models on the road.

Another common practice by parents is to buy a young teen driver something brand new as his or her first vehicle. The idea here is that it will prove more reliable and feature the latest safety devices. The problem is that the first year of driving usually is marked by a fair number of dings, dents and scratches. When this happens to a new vehicle, parents suddenly face two sticky problems:

(1) Who pays for the damages not covered by insurance?

(2) Who pays for the increased insurance premiums triggered by the claim?

I don't recommend buying new vehicles for beginning drivers for exactly these reasons. It's a near certainty that your young driver is going to bang up that first vehicle. When the inevitable happens, what will you do? Will you tell your teen it's okay and shell out the thousands of extra dollars for repairs yourself, thereby relieving him or her of any of the responsibility? Will you require your teen to get a job to work off the expense, paying hard-earned money to a body shop when it could have been better used for college? Or will you simply leave the damage untouched, allowing the metal to rust or the lenses or lights to remain broken? Not very attractive choices, are they?

Let me suggest a better approach: If you must buy something, make it old, large, and solid. My choice, which usually is greeted by groans from teens, is that now-obsolete American classic, the station wagon, preferably one with a small engine.

Station wagons have somewhat stronger frames than sedans. This helps them hold up better in collisions. Another choice would be a full-size sedan, again, with a small engine. Both types of used vehicles should be available within modest budgets. Sure, they tend to guzzle gasoline, but that's an inducement for your teen to keep unnecessary driving to a minimum.

Whatever you do, avoid the temptation to buy something with either a high center of gravity or a powerful engine. The newspapers are full of stories of kids driving flashy cars or SUVs who lost control with tragic consequences. Such fantasy products can wait.

For further information on the subject of vehicle-shopping, check out the recommended books in the "Reviews and Resources" section, on page 173.

I hope you have found all the advice and lessons in this book to be helpful. And I hope you will follow them as long as you drive.

There's one more thing I'd like to mention to you. And I'd like you to think about it very seriously in the coming weeks and months: BE A LIGHTFOOT.

This is something that is related to the five other themes, but is also separate. It means more than just easing off the gas for safety. It also means driving lightly (and quietly) down the roads and streets and neighborhoods. It means being considerate of everyone else around you. It means going easy on the Earth.

This may sound very silly to you. After all, just about everywhere you see driving portrayed — especially on TV and in the movies — speed seems to be the only attitude. It's certainly the prevailing mood on the highways as well.

In fact, driving itself is rarely thought about. Everybody drives everywhere, it seems. Kids reach sixteen and they want to drive. They want their own cars. It's natural, because it means freedom.

But somewhere along the way, this freedom needs to be given more thought. We live in a society that is consuming a huge amount of the Earth's resources. America constitutes less than five percent of the world's population, yet it consumes more than a third of its energy. A huge chunk of that consumption is gasoline for our automobiles.

More and more of our countryside is being appropriated for highways. Several of our largest cities suffer from continuous smog problems. Scientists are concerned about the effects of carbon dioxide emissions on the Earth's atmospheric temperature.

They're also concerned about the damage that oil pollution is doing to the oceans. Part of this damage comes from the large number of ships that transport imported oil to the U.S. and other countries. Most of it, however, results from the steady dripping of oil from the crankcases of every vehicle on Earth. Those drips are washed by the rain into rivers and they eventually end up in the oceans where they are harming the ecosystem.

Then there is the toll of crashes: tens of thousands of fatalities and millions of injuries every year. That's just to people. There are uncounted animals that die by the roadside. Not very pleasant thoughts. But that's what driving on today's American roads really means.

The situation isn't hopeless. Things can be done. You can help — if you are willing to take driving seriously.

First, as anxious as you are to get on the road and exercise your newfound freedom, try, as soon as you can, to drive only when you have to. For example, if you can walk, bike, or take the bus to school every day, do so. Sure, it seems uncool. But every time you leave the car in the driveway, you reduce pollution and energy consumption a little.

Second, whenever you drive (my <u>favorite</u> song by The Cars), drive gently. Be a lightfoot because it reduces fuel consumption.

Last, be especially gentle whenever you drive through neighborhoods, where vehicle noise disturbs the peace and quiet and where speed can kill animals as well as people.

Be a lightfoot, and become a citizen of the Earth.

SOME ABC'S FOR THE ROAD

Here are 23 miscellaneous but noteworthy items to remember, in alphabetical order:

Accidents - I haven't mentioned this word before. That's because what happens on the roads should be called "crashes." If you have one, however, there are several important things to do:

1. Stop. Leaving the scene of a crash is a crime. If you have to, pull out of the way of traffic. But never leave the scene of a crash unless it is a very minor one and all parties agree to do so. When in doubt, stay and wait for the police.

2. Check yourself for injury. If you aren't sure, don't move until a rescue squad arrives.

3. Help anyone else who is injured by applying pressure to bleeding wounds and keeping them warm until help arrives. Do not attempt to move an injured person, however, unless he or she is in danger from fire or moving vehicles.

4. Make sure the crash has been reported to the police.

5. Exchange the following information with the other people involved: name, driver's license number, license plate number and insurance company (including agent's address and policy number). If necessary, try to obtain the name and address of everyone who is injured.

6. Notify your insurance company as soon as possible.

Bump and Mug - A threat to motorists, especially females, that occurs from time to time. If you're driving alone, especially at night, someone might try to bump you from behind, then assault you when you stop.

If this ever happens, keep your doors locked and your windows up. Stay in your car and wait for the police. If no one is around, drive to the nearest police station and report the incident, or to the nearest public place and call the police.

Cigarettes - Don't smoke and drive. You have enough to do behind the wheel without holding a burning object in your hand. It is a hazardous distraction. Besides, smoking is stupid, outside or inside the vehicle.

Drinking and Driving - If you need to be told, you don't belong on the road.

Emotions - Always keep them under control. Be cool behind the wheel. Don't drive when you are angry, and don't get angry when you drive. You could get into a terrible situation. There are lots of extremely immature and volatile people out there who fly into road rage at the slightest provocation. Don't be one of them. There's way too little courtesy on the roads and too much rudeness. Don't add to the problem.

If someone cuts you off or behaves stupidly, don't take it personally. Everybody makes mistakes. Shrug it off. Take a few deep breaths and concentrate on maintaining your cool.

If you're the mistaken one, there's a very effective tool for dealing with the other party: apologize. A nice big gesture that communicates "Sorry!" is the best thing you can do. People may stay angry for a while, but they almost always will cool down if you don't continue to provoke them.

Fatigue - Something every bit as dangerous as alcohol, because it slows your reflexes and dulls your senses. Don't ever think that because you're young, you can't fall victim to fatigue. Exercise the same caution about fatigue that you would about drinking. If you're tired, don't drive. Sleep over or ask for a ride.

Fatigue can strike during the day, too. On long trips, your reflexes can dull over time. Take a short break at least once every two hours. Every four hours, stop and eat something, or take a walk and stretch. And don't drive if you're taking medication, especially antihistamines or sedatives.

Gauges - The order of importance of the three warning gauges on your instrument panel (and your own catchy phrase to remember them):

Boil - First and most important is temperature. When this warning light is on or the gauge moves into the red, it means the temperature of the engine coolant is too high and therefore the engine itself will soon be overheating.

No question, if the instrument panel warns about high temperature, the proper response is to get the vehicle off the road immediately.

If the coolant temperature is too high, it will boil off. You will be able to see steam emerging from the radiator cap. There could be several possible causes. The main thing is that without coolant, the engine practically can self-destruct within a very short time. So it is extremely important to turn off the engine and allow it to cool down. To do so, get the vehicle off the road.

Oil - Next is the oil gauge or warning light. It signifies that the oil level in the crankcase is low. Oil is a critical ingredient in the operation of an engine. Without it, the metal parts inside, many of which are rubbing together up to 100 times a second, would overheat and eventually fuse together.

Engine failure due to oil loss takes longer than failure due to coolant loss. In fact, if the oil light comes on, it usually means that the level is low. Therefore, there is sufficient time to take care of it. Get to a service station.

Coil - This relates to the battery or alternator light or voltage gauge. If trouble is indicated, it means that the battery is not being charged. This is the least urgent of the three warnings. The problem will eventually bring things to a stop, but it doesn't require immediate or emergency attention. The best thing to do is go home.

So remember: Boil/Oil/Coil, in that order.

Highway Workers - They have difficult and dangerous jobs. Slow down whenever you see them and give them plenty of room. If flag persons are directing traffic, follow their instructions and wave thanks to them as you pass by.

Identification - You always need three types when you're driving: driver's license, owner's registration, and proof of insurance. If you're sharing a vehicle, keep your license in your wallet or purse and always make sure the other two documents are in the glove compartment. If it's yours and yours alone, keep all three with you. That way, if the vehicle is stolen, the thief won't have proof of ownership.

Jack - If you're lucky, you'll never have to use one. One way to avoid it is to belong to a roadside assistance organization, which will send out a mechanic. Otherwise, you need to learn the procedure.

Before you begin driving any distance away from home, read your vehicle's instruction manual and learn the entire jacking process. Learn where the lug wrench and jack and spare wheel are stored and how to remove them.

Learn the proper places on the vehicle to mount the jack.

You don't necessarily have to replace a tire if it's very low. You can drive slowly on it (with your emergency flashers on) for several miles until you reach a service station or a parking lot. If this is possible, it's a better situation than the roadside. If you're on a road with a speed limit above 35, drive along the shoulder. If this isn't possible, stay where you are.

The first thing to do is find as level a place as possible that is at least one vehicle width away from the road. Make sure the engine is turned off, the transmission is in park (or first gear) and the parking brake is engaged. Find something — like a rock — to block the opposite wheel to the one you're changing.

Then follow those instructions to the letter.

A caution: if it's dark and lonely, don't do this. Don't expose yourself to careless or predatory motorists. Stay in the vehicle with the doors locked and the windows up. Tie a handkerchief or white cloth to your door handle and wait for the police.

Keys - Keep an extra door key in your wallet, in case you accidentally lock them in the car. Keep your car keys separate from your house keys. If you park in a garage or a lot, and you have to leave your keys with the attendant, you don't want a stranger holding your house keys.

Take your keys with you every time you leave your vehicle, even for a minute. Don't make a thief's job easy. And never leave your vehicle with the engine running. In many jurisdictions, it's a violation.

Locks and Lights - Check them both every time you leave your vehicle. Locks are easy. Before you get out, check the other doors to make sure they're locked. Outside, when you close your door, try the handle.

In the daytime, if the weather is bad and you've been driving with lights on, don't forget to turn them off before you park and leave. Remember that tip I mentioned a while back: get yourself into the habit of looking back at your vehicle after you've walked a few steps away from it. If you do, you'll always see if you've left your lights on.

By the way, turn your headlights on any time the sky darkens, any time you go through a tunnel, and any time you turn your wipers on. Not the parking lights, the head-lights!

Motorcycles - They're different from bicycles because they travel at highway speeds. Treat them with more caution than other vehicles because riders are much more vulnerable. Stay well behind them, and wait for them to go by when you're pulling onto a road.

Necessities - Your vehicle's glove compartment should contain a (working) flashlight, a notepad and pen, a white cloth (in case you need assistance), a stash of quarters (for parking meters and tolls), an extra pair of sunglasses, some napkins or "wet wipes," and a tire pressure gauge.

Elsewhere inside, keep a plastic grocery bag or two under the seat (for litter) and a local area map in case you become lost. You might want to have one of those cardboard windshield sun visors that doubles as an emergency sign.

In the trunk, keep an extra quart of motor oil, a gallon of washer fluid, pints of brake and power steering fluid, an old blanket (in case you ever have to lay on the ground to see under the vehicle), one or two emergency flares, and a small tool kit. It also wouldn't hurt to have a first-aid kit.

In the optional category: a tire reinflation cannister, battery jumper cables and a carburetor/engine quick start chemical. There are drawbacks to having these items, however. They require special handling and knowledge. You instead may want to rely on emergency road service professionals for these contingencies.

Oil and Water - I know, I know, they don't mix. But they are the two most important fluids in your vehicle. You must check them frequently, at least once a week. The best time to do this is when the engine is cold. You need a paper towel or a rag. Draw out the oil dipstick, wipe it clean, and reinsert it all the way. It will be marked so you can tell when to add oil. Use a good multigrade, such as 10W-40.

Keep your vehicle's coolant reservoir filled to the proper level. You can add water or coolant to the expansion tank at any time. But NEVER remove the radiator cap when the engine is hot! Pressure from the system could force boiling fluid or steam through the opening. You and anyone nearby could be scalded.

By the way: in case you haven't learned yet, gasoline can be explosive. Never attempt to refuel your vehicle if anyone nearby is smoking or using a spark or open flame!

Potholes - They can kill your tires and damage other expensive components of your vehicle's suspension. Always avoid them if you can. If you can't, slow down as much as possible before you roll over them.

Don't roll over very rough surfaces while braking (see speedbumps).

Radios/Tape decks/CD players - They are fun and break up the monotony of driving, but they can create hazards in three ways:

1. If you play yours too loudly, it could drown out road sounds that you need to hear, like emergency sirens, approaching trains, or another vehicle's horn.

2. If you focus your attention on changing stations, or on switching a tape or CD, you could miss something critical on the roadway.

3. Loose tapes and discs can do damage to you if they become flying objects in a crash. Keep them in containers that can be stored under seats or in dashboard compartments.

Another by the way: cellular phones also can create problems and dangers. If you have one in the vehicle, be extremely careful when you use it. Talking on the phone while driving can be distracting. New studies have shown that cell phone users are involved in crashes more frequently. While you're still getting used to the road, avoid the added complication. Use the phone only when you're stopped or sitting still in traffic.

Speedbumps - Annoying but necessary things put mostly in parking lots to keep speeds down. Brake first. Slow down before you go over them. Then ease over them, brakes off. They can hurt your suspension, too (see potholes).

Tires - Keep them properly inflated. You can't always tell by looking. Check them when cold, a couple of times a month, according to the pressures recommended in your vehicle's instruction manual.

Vision - Have yours checked periodically. Four out of ten teens suffer from a condition called "night myopia," which affects your eyes' ability to focus in low light. Even if you don't require glasses during the day, you may need them at night.

This is no joke. Teen crashes occur at night four times more frequently than adult crashes.

Wipers and Washers - Wipers wear out frequently. When they do, they create streaks across your windshield. This can be particularly annoying at night. If your wipers are performing poorly, replace the blades immediately. Blades are cheap. Crashes are expensive.

Washer fluid is indispensable for keeping your windshield clean. Check the fluid level often. Keep the reservoir full. Like I said, it's a good idea to keep an extra gallon on board. Fluid is even cheaper than blades.

Zap! - That's the feeling you get when the air is dry and you step out of your vehicle and touch it again. It's caused by the buildup of static electricity.

There's an easy way to avoid this annoyance: whenever you get out of your vehicle, keep touching any metal part of the door until you're outside and standing up. The metal will conduct away any static buildup, so you won't get jolted.

INDEX

A

Acceleration, 83, 86, 88, 89, 96, 99, 102, 114, 115, 127, 129, 134, 135
Accidents, 31, 147 (see "Crashes")
Aggressive drivers, 16, 112, 119, 120, 138
Air conditioning, 25, 125
Airbags, 30, 32
Alcohol, 17, 18, 112, 140, 148
Animals, 33, 49-51, 74, 79, 106
"Ask Phil," 3
Attention, 58, 59, 105, 111, 125
focusing well ahead, 57, 60, 64, 69, 75, 81, 93, 120
varying, 82, 93
Attitude, good driving, 14, 18, 111

B

Backing up, 33, 37, 38, 40, 46, 110
hand position during, 37, 40
Bicyclists, 44, 59, 74, 79, 80, 106
Blind spots, 31, 63, 91, 92
Brake pedal, 25, 37, 39, 41, 43, 47, 50, 61, 67, 74, 121, 129
Braking, 60, 115, 130, 131, 132
antilock, 73, 74, 130, 131, 132
on curves, 73, 75
panic, 73, 134
smooth stops, 43, 61
Bridges, ice on, 135
Brief/Perform/Debrief, 6, 28
Bump and Mug, 148

C

Called stops, 41, 49
'Canyon,' avoiding the, 56, 65, 66
Cellular telephones, 154
Children, 33, 49, 50, 52
Choosing a car for your teen, 143, 144
Cigarettes, 148
CLEAR THE WAY, 7, 33, 37, 45, 46, 57, 60-63, 66, 73, 83, 84, 86-88, 91, 108, 125, 126
CLEAR ZONE, 58-61, 69, 75, 76, 79, 85, 96, 99, 105, 123, 126
Clutch, 25, 26, 67, 136
operation of, 41, 42, 44
Combined speed, 76, 97, 102
Commercial strips, 56, 57, 61, 122, 141
Construction zones, 88, 115, 121
Control, loss of, 70, 73, 129, 134
Control panel, 25, 125
Co-piloting, 27, 28, 61, 67, 97, 107, 141, 142
Courtesy, 14, 90, 96, 114, 118
Crashes
references to, 10, 11, 17, 23, 52, 59, 60, 63, 89, 97, 111-113, 117, 123
teens involved in, 10, 11, 17, 18, 23, 24, 72, 140
what to do in case of, 147
Crosswalks, 44
Curves, 49, 64, 67, 69, 70-76, 81, 96, 101, 105, 124, 127, 129
looking through, 81, 82, 93
slowing down before, 82

D

Death rates for teens, 2, 10, 17, 18
Distances, judging, 64, 76, 82, 87, 91, 117
Door locks, 32, 151, 152
Driver education, 11-12
Drivers' licenses, 11, 12, 139, 142
requirements, 11, 20, 22, 24, 142
Driveways, hidden, 27, 49, 74, 79, 96
Drop-offs, 76-78, 79, 94

E

Ease off the gas, 50, 53, 59, 61, 73, 75-78, 89, 94, 101, 119, 120, 127, 132
Emergency flashers, 95, 96, 101, 123

Emergency stops, 85, 94-96
Emotions, 43, 51, 81, 101, 111, 112,
  114, 148
Empty space, concentrating on the, 45,
  64, 65
Engines, 24
  starting / stopping, 25, 26, 37, 38

F

Fatigue, 21, 111, 141, 148
FEEL THE ROAD, 7, 128, 129
55 m.p.h., 85, 93, 94, 97-100,
  102, 104, 105, 117
  first-year limit of, 85, 93, 94, 111, 140
  on two-lane roads, 96, 97
Fog, 21, 122-125
Following distance, 98, 100,
  101, 112, 114, 115
'F.Re.S.H.,' 131, 132
Friction, 70-72, 124, 127, 134
Fuel gauge, 25

G

Gas pedal, 25, 26, 39, 41, 42, 47,
  67, 74, 99, 129
Gauges, 25
  Boil / Oil / Coil, 149, 150
Gearshift, 25, 26, 29, 37, 38, 136

H

Hazard-spotting, 27, 28, 49, 52,
  54, 57, 59, 61, 67
Headlights, 25, 54, 89, 91-93, 98,
  102, 103-105
  overdriving, 103, 105
  turning off, 103, 106, 107, 151
  turning on, 103, 104, 122
Headrests, adjusting, 32
Highway workers, 121, 150
Highways

center turn lane, 84
  easing onto, 85, 95, 96
  entering, 85, 89, 97
  exiting, 85, 86, 88, 89, 97
  four-lane, 85, 91, 96, 111, 115, 142
  two-lane, 67, 76, 85, 96-101, 103, 111, 113, 140
Hills, 49, 50, 67, 69, 70, 72, 75,
  76, 89, 96, 101, 105, 137
Horn, using the, 51, 53, 79

I

Ice, 121, 128-130, 134, 135
'Ice Cream,' 105, 106, 126
Identification, 149
Impatient drivers, 27, 43, 51, 111
  never hold up, 101, 114
Inconsistencies, 58, 105, 106, 126
Inertia, 70-72, 134
Insurance Institute for Highway
  Safety, 10, 23, 160
Intersections, 33, 44, 56, 57, 60, 61-65,
  83, 98, 107, 109

J

Jack, using the, 150, 151

K

Keys, 142, 151

L

Lanes
  changing, 56, 59, 62, 63, 114, 119
  holding, 47, 57, 61, 76, 81, 93, 108, 115, 120, 121
  left, 89-91, 101
  narrow, 45, 54, 107, 108, 115, 121
  right, 56, 61, 90
  staying within, 39, 41, 57, 64, 82, 93
LEARN THE LIMITS, 7, 70-74, 128
Learner's permit, 20
  state requirements, 20, 23, 24

Lesson Log, 163-172
LIGHTFOOTING, 113, 114, 144, 145
Limits, post-license, 111, 115, 130,
   139, 140

M
Maps, using, 66
Merging, 85-88, 115-118, 141
   entrance ramps, 86, 87, 115-117
   exit ramps, 88, 89, 94
   'let 'em in,' 89, 118, 119
   merge slots, 87, 116, 119
   mixing loops, 117, 118
   stopping on ramps, 87, 116, 117
Mirrors
   adjusting, 31, 36, 37
   using, 38, 57, 58, 63, 81, 82,
   84, 87, 91, 102, 119
Motorcycles, 152

N
Necessities, 152, 153

O
Oil and water, 153
Oncoming vehicles, 45, 46, 76,
   97, 98, 103, 104, 109, 116, 127
   One-way streets, 107, 111
Owner's manual, 25

P
Parallel parking, 44, 108-111
Parking brake, 26, 29, 37, 38
Parking drills, 37, 38, 46, 47
Parking garages, 54, 122
   personal safety in, 54, 55
   tap the wall, 55, 94
Parking lots, 42
   empty, 29, 36, 41, 122, 129-134
   shopping center, 51, 53
Parking spaces
   positioning inside, 38, 39
   pulling into and out of, 33, 37-
   41, 45, 46, 51, 52, 54, 62

Passengers, dangers of, 2, 140, 142
Passing, 67, 85, 91, 101-103, 115
   being passed, 85, 92, 93, 98,
   100, 113, 114
   by trucks, 85, 92, 93, 104, 105,
   on right, 119
   on two-lane roads, 98, 101-103
Pedestrians, 37, 44, 49, 52, 59, 65,
   74, 80, 106, 107
Peripheral vision, 58, 67, 93
Post-license check-ups, 141
Potholes, 27, 59, 106, 153
Predictability, 57, 64, 89, 99, 114
Pre-drive checklist, 30, 36, 41, 43

R
Radios/tape decks/CD players, 153,
   154
Railroad crossings, 74, 80, 81
Rain, 21, 121-124, 128, 130, 134
Reacting, 50, 57, 68, 118
Red light runners, 57, 62, 65
Refueling, 25, 34, 152
Road signs, 58, 67, 83, 106, 107
Roads
   contour of, 69, 74
   flooded, 124, 127, 128
   getting back on, 83, 84
   ice and snow on, 72, 130, 134-136
   substances on, 72, 127
   water on, 72, 123, 127, 128

S
Seatbelts, 30, 36, 140
Seats, adjusting, 30, 36
SHARE THE ROAD, 7, 79, 80, 89,
   93, 96, 99, 100, 118
Shifting, 42-44, 49, 67, 74-76,
   97, 99
   frequent, 74-76
   tip for, 44
Skids, 70-73, 124, 130-136
   'F.Re.S.H.,' 131, 132
   power, 134-136

test the road, 135, 136
Slowing down, 76, 114, 123
  for curves, 71, 72, 82
  for hazards, 45, 50, 51, 53, 69,
  73, 79, 94, 95
  for turns, 56, 89, 99, 134
Snow, 21, 121, 124, 128, 130,
  134, 136, 137
Speed, 39, 42, 43, 49, 56, 59, 60,
  67, 69, 70, 76, 82, 85, 92-94,
  100, 103, 105, 111-114, 123,
  129, 131, 134-136, 140
  adjusting, 67, 75, 126
  checking, 69, 93
  combined, 76, 97, 102
  maintaining steady, 39, 57, 61,
  75, 86, 93, 100
Speedbumps, 29, 154
Static electricity, 155
Steering, 39, 74, 131, 132
  hands follow the eyes, 39, 68, 75,
  120
Steering wheel, 37, 39, 47, 48, 129
  adjusting the, 32, 36
  gripping the, 32
Stop lights, 49, 56, 60, 96, 109, 125,
  approaching, 57, 61
  caution before starting from, 57,
  60, 62
Stopping distance, 59, 60, 69, 85,
  96, 100, 124, 126, 127
  Three-Second Rule, 65, 100
Stop signs, 33, 44, 45, 60, 61,
  88, 125

T

Tachometers, 97
Tailgaters, 51, 81, 98, 101, 113
Teaching, 26-29
  Brief / Perform / Debrief, 6, 28
  instructional methods, 26-29, 35,
  36, 39, 51, 52, 63
  learning by doing, 26
  pointing out mistakes, 28
THINK AHEAD, 7, 107-109, 116

Tires, 95, 129, 151, 154
  friction / loss of, 70-73, 127,
  131, 134
  hydroplaning of, 127
  inflation, 25, 154
  wear on, 40
Tractors and farm machinery, 74,
  78, 79, 98
Traffic, 51, 52, 56-61, 64, 65,
  67, 78, 84, 86, 88, 90, 100,
  101, 104, 107-109, 111-113,
  115-122, 127, 140, 142
  clogs, 107, 109, 115, 120
  'keeping up with,' 112, 113
  lane weavers, 119
  packs, 112-115
Trucks, 57, 65, 88, 92, 104,
  105,
  107, 108, 126, 127
Turnarounds, 47, 48
Turns
  hand position during, 39
  left, 56, 62-64, 84, 109
  off of highways, 56, 99
  onto highways, 83, 98
  right, 44, 56, 62, 66
  signaling before, 39, 45, 56,
  59, 63, 64, 89, 91, 95, 99
  Two-Second Rule after, 65
Turn signals, 25, 63, 86, 88, 95,
  96, 100-102, 116, 118

V

Visibility, 30, 33, 69, 70, 78, 79,
  83, 84, 97, 122
Vision, 123, 124, 126, 154

W

Web sites, 3, 173, 174
Windows, clean, 125
Windshield, 125
  cleaning, 34, 36
  defogger, 122, 124, 125
  wipers and washers, 25, 34,
  122, 124, 126, 154, 155

ACKNOWLEDGMENTS

This book began as an article that appeared in *The Washington Post* and *Pittsburgh Post-Gazette* in the fall of 1994. It originated in the wake of a terrible and notorious crash involving several teenagers in the Washington D.C. suburbs. My intention at the time was to encourage parents to become more actively involved in their teens' instruction. Using my experiences with my own children, I tried to explain how, with patience and care, they could teach solid basic skills and a mature attitude.

In the months that followed, many parents who had heard about the article continued to request reprints of it. During the winter of 1996, I participated in a meeting of the Parent Teachers Association in Arlington Virginia on the subject of the current state of driving instruction for youngsters. Afterward, quite a few parents approached me and expressed appreciation for the article. Several told me that they had adopted all my recommendations when they taught their teens to drive. Based on those responses, I decided to expand the article into a book.

I'd like to thank Peggy Hackman, editor of the *Post's* "Style Plus" section, for her help with the original article and her initial suggestions about the book. Tom O'Boyle, managing editor of the *Post-Gazette*, also was very supportive of my work.

Evelyn Metzger, owner of EPM Publications, my original publisher, was receptive and enthusiastic about the book idea from the beginning. Now in semi-retirement, she remains a pioneer in the publishing field. She was a joy to work with, as was her hardworking staff; likewise her skilled designer (and my fellow Time-Life alumnus), Tom Huestis.

Among the people who reviewed the manuscript, some were parents who have used the material to teach their teens. Thanks especially to Judy Hadden, of the Arlington County PTA, for her support and comments.

Stephen L. Oesch, General Counsel, and Dr. Allan F. Williams, Senior Vice President for Research, both of the Insurance Institute for Highway Safety, provided valuable critiques of the manuscript, as well as important statistics about teen drivers and crashes.

My two former housemates, Rick Hurd and Sandi Holt, lent unlimited moral support and patience during my months of laboring to write the manuscript. My good friends, Dick Schwartzbard, and Dr. Rosemary Schwartzbard, reviewed the manuscript and provided useful suggestions. Another close friend, Barbara Freeman, interrupted her dinner preparations one night to take the photograph of me and my daughters on the following page.

I can't say enough about my publisher, publicist, partner and friend, Katherine Hutt, of Nautilus Communications. The success that this book now enjoys is largely due to her tireless labor, support and enthusiasm. Also, many thanks to Claire Liston, VP of Creative Services at Nautilus, for her superb work in keeping our Web site looking great and up to date.

I am especially grateful to my dear father, F.A. Berardelli, for applying his skilled pen to the illustrations that accompany the text.

Last but not least, Jessie Thorpe, the finest writer I know, continues to encourage and help me in my efforts. To her, my thanks and enduring affection.

The author and his daughters

ABOUT THE AUTHOR

Phil Berardelli is a writer and journalist with more than 25 years of experience. He has covered such topics as energy, science, education and popular culture, as well as highway safety. His work has appeared in *The Washington Post, Los Angeles Times, Pittsburgh Post-Gazette*, and other newspapers and magazines.

Currently, he is senior writer at www.ThinkNet.org, a consortium of educational consultants and developers.

His background also includes seven years as a middle school teacher, and five years as producer and co-host of the weekly television program, "The Moviegoing Family," which appeared in the Washington, D.C. area and nationally on The Learning Channel.

Born in Pittsburgh, Pennsylvania, he has lived in Northern Virginia since 1970.

SAFE YOUNG DRIVERS LESSON LOG

LESSON #	DATE	STEP #	LENGTH (HRS.)	SKILLS LEARNED	PROBLEMS	NOTES

SAFE YOUNG DRIVERS LESSON LOG

LESSON #	DATE	STEP #	LENGTH (HRS.)	SKILLS LEARNED	PROBLEMS	NOTES

SAFE YOUNG DRIVERS LESSON LOG

LESSON #	DATE	STEP #	LENGTH (HRS.)	SKILLS LEARNED	PROBLEMS	NOTES

SAFE YOUNG DRIVERS LESSON LOG

LESSON #	DATE	STEP #	LENGTH (HRS.)	SKILLS LEARNED	PROBLEMS	NOTES

SAFE YOUNG DRIVERS LESSON LOG

LESSON #	DATE	STEP #	LENGTH (HRS.)	SKILLS LEARNED	PROBLEMS	NOTES

SAFE YOUNG DRIVERS LESSON LOG

LESSON #	DATE	STEP #	LENGTH (HRS.)	SKILLS LEARNED	PROBLEMS	NOTES

SAFE YOUNG DRIVERS LESSON LOG

LESSON #	DATE	STEP #	LENGTH (HRS.)	SKILLS LEARNED	PROBLEMS	NOTES

SAFE YOUNG DRIVERS LESSON LOG

LESSON #	DATE	STEP #	LENGTH (HRS.)	SKILLS LEARNED	PROBLEMS	NOTES

SAFE YOUNG DRIVERS LESSON LOG

LESSON #	DATE	STEP #	LENGTH (HRS.)	SKILLS LEARNED	PROBLEMS	NOTES

SAFE YOUNG DRIVERS LESSON LOG

LESSON #	DATE	STEP #	LENGTH (HRS.)	SKILLS LEARNED	PROBLEMS	NOTES

REVIEWS

"One of the best investments you'll make in your child's life... This is a book that every parent trying to teach a teenager to drive ought to read. This is not just a safe-driving manual: It is about the relationship between parents and teenagers and how teaching our children to drive can strengthen that relationship. It is also about the relationship we have with other drivers... and that's a notion that mindlessly aggressive 'adult' drivers could contemplate as well."

— **Judy Mann**, Columnist, *The Washington Post*

"The book is clearly the product of a man who not only has affection and understanding for young people, but also for cars and driving... Berardelli provides clear, well-considered advice, organized in a way that lets the author speak plainly with both parents and teens... Obviously, this is a man who has been there. *Safe Young Drivers* is a recommended resource for any parent; I'll use it in teaching my own teens."

— **Kevin A. Wilson**, Executive Editor, *AutoWeek*

"*Safe Young Drivers* is divided into separate sections for parents and teens... filled with facts and advice about everything you'd want your child to know about safe driving, as well as specific safe-driving actions and the consequences for lapses in good sense... Thanks to Berardelli's exhaustive effort, even experienced drivers are likely to learn something new."

— *GEICO Today*

"You would benefit from this book even if your child is going through a pubic school driver ed. program or a {commercial} course, because what this book addresses is *how* to actually help your child once you two are out there in that vehicle... The book is a gem."

— **Susan Richman**, Pennsylvania Homeschoolers

RESOURCES

✳ Information about your state's rules for learner's permits and licenses is available from your local Department of Motor Vehicles office. That's also where you can obtain a copy of your state's driving manual. If you don't know the nearest DMV location, try the American Association of Motor Vehicle Administrators (AAMVA) Web site: www.aamva.org. From there, you can find every DMV and state police Web site in the U.S. and Canada.

✳ Help in the fight against drinking and driving is available from Mothers Against Drunk Driving. The organization can be reached by calling 1-800-GET-MADD, or through its Web site: www.madd.org.

✳ Additional information, as well as opportunities for teen involvement, is available from SADD (Students Against Destructive Decisions). SADD can be reached by phone at 1-508-481-3568, or on the Web at www.nat-sadd.org. SADD also has a "Contract For Life" between teens and adults that can be useful in the driving instruction process. The teen promises to forego the use of alcohol or drugs, not to ride with anyone who has been using, to always wear seat belts, and not to hesitate to call whenever an unsafe situation has arisen. The adult promises, among other things, to provide safe and sober transportation home whenever needed.

✳ Further information on the subject of vehicle-shopping is available from the following sources:

Buying a Safer Car, a brochure that explains government safety tests and lists test results for many popular models; and *New Car Safety Features*, a brochure that explains the newest safest features, are available from the National Highway Traffic Safety Administration. Call (toll-free) 1-888-DASH-2-DOT, or find them on the Web: www.nhtsa.dot.gov.

Shopping for a Safer Car, a brochure that rates vehicle crashworthiness based on real-world insurance claims. It's available from the Insurance Institute for Highway Safety. Telephone: 703-247-1500 Web: www.highwaysafety.org

The Car Book and *The Used Car Book*, both by Jack Gillis and both updated annually. They are available in bookstores or from Amazon.com. Mr. Gillis is Director of Public Affairs for the Consumer Federation of America and consumer correspondent for NBC's "Today Show." He is widely recognized as the most trustworthy car expert in the business, and his books are quite consumer-friendly.

✳ Information about the national campaign to adopt graduated licensing is available in a booklet called *Saving Teenage Lives: The Case for Graduated Driver Licensing*. Published by the National Highway Traffic Safety Administration, it provides basic facts on graduated driver licensing laws, how this approach saves lives, and success stories from the U.S. and other countries. It also offers a model law, as well as ideas on how to generate support for similar policies in your state. The booklet can be ordered online at www.nhtsa.dot.gov or by calling 888-DASH-2-DOT. Ask for publication DOT HS 808-801 (Item #2P1043).